SUÁREZ

MESSI

NEYMAR

About the author

Luca Caioli is the bestselling author of the biographies *Messi*, *Ronaldo*, *Neymar* and *Suárez*, all published by Icon Books. A renowned Italian sports journalist, he lives in Spain.

SUÁREZ MESSI NEYMAR

INSIDE BARCELONA'S
UNSTOPPABLE
NEW STRIKEFORCE

LUCA CAIOLI

ICON

Published in the UK and USA in 2014 by
Icon Books Ltd, Omnibus Business Centre,
39–41 North Road, London N7 9DP
email: info@iconbooks.com
www.iconbooks.com

Sold in the UK, Europe and Asia
by Faber & Faber Ltd, Bloomsbury House,
74–77 Great Russell Street, London WC1B 3DA or their agents

Distributed in the UK, Europe and Asia
by TBS Ltd, TBS Distribution Centre, Colchester Road
Frating Green, Colchester CO7 7DW

Distributed in Australia and New Zealand
by Allen & Unwin Pty Ltd, PO Box 8500,
83 Alexander Street, Crows Nest, NSW 2065

Distributed in South Africa
by Jonathan Ball, Office B4, The District,
41 Sir Lowry Road, Woodstock 7925

Distributed in India by Penguin Books India,
7th Floor, Infinity Tower – C, DLF Cyber City,
Gurgaon 122002, Haryana

Distributed in Canada by Publishers Group Canada,
76 Stafford Street, Unit 300
Toronto, Ontario M6J 2S1

Distributed to the trade in the USA by
Consortium Book Sales and Distribution,
The Keg House, 34 Thirteenth Avenue NE,
Suite 101, Minneapolis, Minnesota 55413-1007

ISBN: 978-190685-086-9

Typeset in New Baskerville by Marie Doherty

Printed and bound in the UK by Clays Ltd, St Ives plc

Contents

Introduction

Suárez, Messi and Neymar ... 9, 10 and 11 ... FC Barcelona's lucky numbers. They are widely considered to be the most powerful strike force in the world, the holy trinity that will rescue the Blue and Clarets from the depths of the 2013-14 season. What's more, the club that has dominated the last decade of European football is now betting on an entirely South American trio. Meanwhile, eternal rival Real Madrid has taken the polar opposite approach with an equally magnificent formation of three players born and trained in Europe: Portuguese Cristiano Ronaldo, Frenchman Karim Benzema and Welshman Gareth Bale.

Of course, Leo Messi is homegrown. Barça is his first and only team, at least for now. Back in his hometown in Argentina he played briefly for Newell's Old Boys in the youth leagues, but he moved over to join Barcelona's youth academy while he was still a boy. He has come up through the ranks of La Masia, and he knows the playing style, what the club represents, its aspirations. But he has also inherited the Latin American culture of playground and street football and all its traditions. It's a 'bilingual' background that can only benefit his relationship with his two new teammates.

He has already been playing with Neymar Júnior for a year, but it has been a particularly difficult twelve months. Legal scandals and injuries have taken their toll on both players. And let's not forget that it's the Brazilian's first taste of football outside his home country and only his second team after Santos, so it's only natural that there has been a period of adjustment. But the fans can breathe easily – since the start of the 2014-15 season there have been signs of a greater understanding between the two, which can only mean a strong and more dangerous Barça.

And as if Leo and Ney weren't enough, enter Luis Suárez, this year's big gamble for the club. An explosive player in every sense – from his performance and his desire to win, to his temperament. 'Lucho', as he is known, has been the most talked about transfer of the season. His move to Barça comes just days after the biting of Italian Giorgio Chiellini during the Brazil World Cup. The result: a nine-match ban at international level and a four-month ban. Suárez apologised publicly prior to his move to Barcelona, but after the deal was announced there were mutterings that the Uruguayan would not be a good fit for the Catalan team's values. Whatever his flaws, there is no denying his abilities, which have made him one of

Uruguay's top players – and one of the best paid. It will be important to see how he fits in with Messi and Ney, and how they, in turn, welcome him into the fold. He will have to demonstrate once again his versatility and capacity to adapt. This is one of his greatest strengths, which made him an indispensable player in all of his former teams: Montevideo's Nacional, Groningen, Ajax and Liverpool. He is well versed in historic clubs and demanding tournaments such as the Premier League, and his wealth of experience should ease his integration into the Catalan club – and into Messi and Neymar territory.

The three players have very differing physiques and abilities. Suárez represents strength, Neymar is technically skilful, while Messi, as the winner of four Ballon d'Ors, has it all. If this gamble taken by new Barça coach Luis Enrique pays off, it could be the beginning of another golden age for the club, like the Guardiola years. The statistics look promising: between them they have nearly 900 official matches under their belt for their various clubs and countries. They are all natural goal-scorers, used to winning prizes and breaking one record after another. It's incredible considering Luis and Lionel are only 27, and Neymar is just 22. They have all enjoyed immense success so far, so it will be interesting to follow their progress over the next few years with the Blaugrana ('Blue and Clarets', as Barça are known in Catalan).

Their triumphs on the pitch have also made them genuine idols, global icons on the level of rock stars or Hollywood actors, followed by millions. They stir up a frenzy both on and off the pitch and their faces and shirts are among the biggest sellers worldwide. Everything they do is heavily scrutinised and their personal lives are the subject of as much fascination as their sporting achievements – fuelled further every time they post a picture of themselves with their partners or children on one of their various social media pages. They are more than just sportsmen: they are wizards with the ball, but they are also extremely bankable public figures across every conceivable market. They are 21st-century footballers – as successful commercially as they are on the pitch.

This is the tale of three kids who knew from an early age that they wanted to be the best, and stopped at nothing to achieve their goals. There are surprising similarities in their parallel stories, which have now finally converged. Here we recount their childhood, family life, first brush with football, club successes, national careers, and key moments of triumph and pain. The chapters that follow offer an insight into three exceptional sportsmen – fierce, tireless warriors. Numbers 9, 10 and 11, the three magic numbers, the three stars of FC Barcelona.

Chapter 1

The scouts

Luis Suárez, Leo Messi and Neymar Júnior almost certainly wouldn't be global football stars if not for the people who discovered them. Or at least, the road to success would have been significantly longer. Because it's not enough just to have great skills. Becoming a football star is as much about being lucky enough to get noticed – having someone recognise your potential even while you're still a youngster playing a childhood game. Here we pay tribute to the three people who 'discovered' the three Barça forwards.

* * *

El Cabeza or Cabezón – 'Big Head', as Suárez's friends and family call him – owes a lot to his paternal uncle, Sergio 'El Chango' Suárez. He was the one who taught him how to kick a ball at four years of age, when Luis was the Deportivo Artigas mascot. El Chango lived in a modest, low-rise house in Salto, in Barrio Cerro. Despite the rundown nature of the area, the locals took pride in their surroundings.

El Chango is shy. He works as a carpenter, but he previously played for amateur Uruguayan teams Deportivo, Fénix and Colombia – a couple of which are now defunct. When asked what Luis was like back then, his uncle smiles. 'He was just like he is now. Football was everything to him. He woke up with a football and went to bed with one.' He paints a picture of a strong player with a constant desire to improve. 'At first Luis was a bit awkward with the ball, but he committed to every shot. He never left a play unfinished. He wanted to win. He wanted to score, he wanted to be the goal-scorer, whatever it took. Just as he does now.'

Is it really possible that one of the most prolific strikers in Premier League history was so clumsy as a child? 'He was better in defence, so much so that when we played against tough opponents, I put him in goal,' admits Sergio. 'He didn't like that but he did his best. He saved the day on many occasions.'

It is difficult to imagine Barcelona's latest star signing as a goalie, but El Chango has proof in the form of a plastic bag bulging with mementos. With a smile just like his nephew's, the greying, bespectacled uncle flips through the photos. There is the Deportivo Artigas kids' team with Luis in front of goal, there are photos of the kids lined up with arms folded and serious expressions, staring into the lens – just like adult players do before a big match. They are wearing red with white and blue stripes and light blue shorts. 'The strip is pretty much the same as that of Independiente Argentino,' notes Sergio. It's hard to spot Luis. 'You should recognise him here,' he says, pointing out a dark, scruffy-haired kid with a cheeky smile They are lined up in order of height at the edge of the tufty grass pitch. Sergio is also visible – considerably younger, with dark brown hair, busy lining them up. Luis is third along with shorts that are too big for him, holding back a smile.

Another picture shows Luis in goal, with a haircut reminiscent of the Beatles. This time he's in an orange strip, standing in the second row with his hands behind his back, right next to his uncle who is trying to get a kid in front of him to stop fidgeting. The trip down memory lane brings back plenty of memories. One of the best is when, 'in the middle of a match, Luis raised his hand and asked the referee to stop play so he could go to the toilet. Another one is when he was five years old. He was playing when he saw his brother, Paolo, in the crowd, eating a piping hot pizza. Luis kicked the ball into touch and ran to Paolo to get a slice. Paolo told him to get back on the pitch but Luis was having none of it. Luis was yelling, he wanted the pizza. Typical boyish antics. Luis was a good kid, just like he is now.'

Luis has always acknowledged that it was his uncle who taught him to kick a ball, but El Chango is

reluctant to take any credit: 'I didn't teach him anything. He already had the basics. What he has achieved
is all down to him.'

It's a very different picture from the one painted by
Braian Rodríguez, a striker with Spanish second division team CD Numancia, who also played at Deportivo
Artigas as a kid. 'El Chango taught us to love football
and to live it with passion. This was important advice
which, as a kid, stays with you for the rest of your life.
He taught us how to move on the pitch and caress the
ball. He explained how to kick, tackle, free yourself
from markers and finish off a move. He taught us that
football is a team game and that there is no point playing for yourself, that passing is key. All of these things
are counterintuitive when you are a kid. He was a great
teacher. Without his help, we may not have made it to
where we are today.'

* * *

Leo Messi may not have made it to the top if Salvador
Ricardo Aparicio hadn't believed in him when he
was just a boy. Aparicio has worked his whole life on
the railways. As a youngster he wore the number 4
shirt for Club Fortín and, more than 30 years ago,
he coached children on Grandoli's pitch. 'I needed
one more to complete the team of children born in
1986. I was waiting for the final player with the shirt
in my hands while the others were warming up. But

he didn't show up, and there was this little kid kicking the ball against the stands,' recalls Don Apa, as he is affectionately known in Leo's hometown of Rosario. The former coach continues: 'The cogs were turning and I said to myself, damn … I don't know if he knows how to play but … So I went to speak to the boy's grandmother, who was really into football, and I said to her: "Lend him to me." She wanted to see him on the pitch. She had asked me many times to let him try out. On many occasions she would tell me about all the little guy's talents. The mother, or the aunt, I can't remember which, didn't want him to play: "He's so small, the others are all huge." To reassure her I told her: I'll stand him over here, and if they attack him I'll stop the game and take him off." Well … I gave him the shirt and he put it on. The first ball came his way, he looked at it and … nothing.' Why? 'He's left-footed, that's why he didn't get to the ball.' He goes on: 'The second it came to his left foot, he latched onto it, and went past one guy, then another and another. I was yelling at him: "Kick it, kick it." He was terrified someone would hurt him but he kept going and going. I don't remember if he scored the goal – I had never seen anything like it. I said to myself: "That one's never coming off." And I never took him off.'

Like El Chango, Aparicio also keeps a bag full of precious memories from the old days. He rummages among the pictures until he finds his favourite: a green pitch, a team of kids wearing red shirts and, standing just in front of a rather younger-looking Don Apa, the smallest of them all – the white trousers almost reaching his armpits, the shirt too large, the expression very serious, bowlegged. It's Leo. He looks like a little bird, like a flea, as his brother Rodrigo used to call him.

'He was born in '87 and he played with the '86 team. He was the smallest in stature and the youngest, but he really stood out. And they punished him hard, but he was a distinctive player, with supernatural talent. He was born knowing how to play. When we would go to a game, people would pile in to see him. When he got the ball he destroyed it. He was unbelievable, they couldn't stop him. He scored four or five goals a game. He scored one, against the Club de Amanecer, which was the kind you see in adverts. I remember it well: he went past everyone, including the keeper. What was his playing style? The same as it is now – free. What was he like? He was a serious kid, he always stayed quietly by his grandmother's side. He never complained. If they hurt him he would cry sometimes but he would get up and keep running. That's why I argue with everyone, I defend him, when they say that he's too much of a soloist, or that he's nothing special, or that he's greedy.'

The first time Leo came home from Spain, Don Apa went to visit him. 'It was madness. I went in the morning and when I returned it was one o'clock the next morning. We spent the whole time chatting about what football was like over there in Spain.' On another occasion, when the neighbourhood organised a party in Lionel's honour, the old maestro didn't get to see his former pupil as Leo wasn't able to make it. He called later to apologise, with a promise to see him next time. Señor Aparicio holds no bitterness – on the contrary, he speaks with much affection about the little boy he coached all those years ago. 'When I saw on TV the first goal he scored in a Barcelona shirt I started to cry. My daughter Genoveva, who was in the other room, asked: "What's wrong dad?" "Nothing," I said, "it's emotional."'

* * *

Roberto Antônio 'Betinho' dos Santos's story is rather different to the other two: discovering Neymar Júnior changed his life. 'In 2002 when Santos tried to coax Neymar Júnior away from the team but without me, Neymar Pai did not accept. He said, "My son needs Betinho at the moment." When Santos tried again and managed to agree a contract, Neymar Pai insisted that I went to Santos with Neymar Júnior. I have Neymar Pai to thank for my job,' he recalls with a smile. The São Vicente native and former amateur right winger still travels the length and breadth of Brazil – and the world – in search of new talent. He has always had a good eye for spotting a diamond in the rough. In

1990 he saw São Vicente five-aside club Beira-Mar and discovered Robson de Souza, aka Robinho, the former Real Madrid, Manchester City and AC Milan forward who is now on loan to Santos.

But the Neymar story is particularly exceptional. 'It was the end of 1998 and I was watching a match on Itararé beach in São Vicente. I was distracted by my son – I turned round to see where he had got to, and I noticed a tiny kid, with short hair and skinny legs. He was running up and down the makeshift stands they had put up for the event. He was running with total ease, as though he were running on a completely flat surface, no obstacles. That's what stood out for me. It was like a light bulb moment.' At the end of the match the scout asked the father's permission to let him try out at Tumiaru. Neymar Pai agreed. 'The first time I saw him touch a ball, my heart started beating like mad,' recalls Betinho. 'I saw the footballing genius that he could become.'

But what were Neymar's talents at that young age? 'Football was an innate ability for him. He already had his own style, even at six years of age. He had speed and balance and he invented imaginative tricks of his own. He loved to dribble, he knew how to shoot and he wasn't afraid of his opponents. He was different from the others, you could put him in the midst of 200 other kids his age, and even then he would shine.' Betinho continues: 'What was lacking was strength and stamina, which is completely normal for a kid at that age. He needed to refine and improve his skills and technique, by playing in a team but without losing his passion for dribbling.'

Betinho took 'Juninho' – as Neymar's family call him – with him to teams where he coached: Portuguesa, Gremetal and a second spell at Portuguesa. 'Neymar was different: he was a very intelligent player. He thought quickly, his mind saw things before the others did. He was always one step ahead. He knew where the ball would end up and how his opponent would react. He took on board my advice and that of the other coaches, and put it into practice. He was the first to arrive at training and the last to leave the pitch. He loved playing with the ball.'

But what sort of six-year-old was he? 'He was a happy little boy, always cheery, always smiling. He had a nice way about him. He was good at school and he liked studying. He got on well with adults and classmates alike. He was friends with everyone and a born leader. His mates trusted him because of what he could do on the pitch. I am very proud of the fact that I was the first coach of a player that is now known all over the world.'

Chapter 2

Football: a passion since childhood

Why do you love football so much?

'I don't know. I first took a liking to it as a child, as all children do, and I still enjoy it a lot. For me, playing ball is one of the most beautiful things in the world.'

It's true, football has been Leo Messi's greatest love since he was a little boy – although it wasn't his first. At three years old, Leo prefers picture cards and much smaller balls – marbles. He wins multitudes of them from his playmates and his bag is always full. At nursery or at school there is always time to play with round objects. Then, for his fourth birthday, his parents give him a white ball with red diamonds, and it is then, perhaps, that the fatal attraction begins. One day he surprises everyone. His father and brothers are playing in the street and Leo decides to join the game for the first time. On many other occasions he had preferred to keep winning marbles – but not this time. 'We were stunned when we saw what he could do,' says his father, Jorge Messi. 'He had never played before.'

From that moment on, he and his football are inseparable. 'He was a typically shy child and he talked very little. He only stood out when he played ball. I remember that at break time in the school playground the captains who had to pick the teams always ended up arguing because they all wanted Leo, because he scored so many goals. With him they were sure to win. Football has always been his passion. He often used to miss birthday parties in order to go to a match or a practice,' recalls his childhood friend Cintia Arellano. And when asked today how he gained such confidence and learned so many tricks, the Flea replies: 'By spending every moment with a football. When I was little I would stand all on my own on a corner and kick the ball around continuously.'

At barely five years of age he begins to get a taste for goals and success at the Grandoli ground under the direction of his first coach, Don Apa. In the second year, he is even lucky enough to have his old man as his coach. Jorge Messi accepts the offer from the club's directors and takes charge of the '87 team. They play against Alfi, one of their many fixtures across the city. And they win everything: 'But everything, everything: the championship, the tournaments, the friendlies …' recalls Jorge, with more paternal pride than that of a coach. But Leo will never forget the person who has been there since the beginning, and who played a key role in his love of football: 'My grandmother

Celia took me to the ground the first time. She was a very important person, very special to all of us. She was such a good person. I remember Sundays at her house being something of a party.'

And if the ball is an extension of his body, Rosario club Newell's Old Boys is part of his DNA. It's his family's team – his father played there from the age of thirteen until he began his military service. A midfielder with a great eye for the game, more defensive than attacking, although he never made it to professional level. Rodrigo, Leo's oldest brother, joined their football school aged seven, and middle brother Matías followed in his footsteps.

It seems only natural that Leo should continue the family tradition. The club scouts know about him. They have asked his brothers to bring him along to find out if he really is extraordinary, which is how the youngest Messi brother ends up playing eight games in as many different formations in the minor leagues, during afternoons and evenings over the course of almost a month for the club. It is an intense test and he does not disappoint. The Newell's coaches think he is phenomenal and recommend him for the Escuela de Fútbol Malvinas (Malvinas School of Football), which nurtures particularly young players. He is not yet seven years old. The club's directors have to consult with the parents first, but given their family passion for football there is no problem.

And so, on 21 March 1994, Lionel Andrés Messi, ID number 992312, becomes a member of Club Atlético Newell's Old Boys. They win numerous titles in the youth leagues and rack up more than 100 goals a season, earning them the nickname *la Máquina del '87* – the '87 Machine. And little Messi captures the attention of the media with, among other things, his tricks with the ball. During training and before matches, he would play 'keepy-uppy' for his own amusement, and before long he is asked to entertain the public during the half-time break of the first team's matches. They announce his name over the speakers and he goes down through the stands doing tricks and then positions himself in the centre of the pitch, where he performs wonders with the ball. It is half-time entertainment that many Newell's fans still remember.

* * *

Luis Suárez's obsession with football also began at a young age. 'He played football in front of his house with his brothers. He played non-stop,' recalls Gladys, an elderly neighbour of the Suárez Díaz family. At four or five years of age he tags along with his eleven-year-old brother Paolo to give the older boys a run for their money. Matches go on for hours, interrupted only by dinner. Even at home, the kids find a way to continue playing, heading and doing keepy-uppy. On one occasion Luis breaks his parents' bed. Anywhere is fair game: at home, in the street and on the dusty patches of land. And then there is 'baby football' – an extremely popular sport for kids in Uruguay, which involves lively games on small pitches and lots of contact with the ball – the perfect way to gain plenty of confidence before moving up to the bigger pitches.

'As a goalie he was pretty good,' recalls his old Deportivo teammate Braian Rodríguez. 'And on the pitch he was fast, decisive, just like his dad, able to skim past two or three opponents. Our Baby Deportivo team was virtually unbeaten. Nobody wanted to play against us. When he was seven, Luis left for Montevideo with his family and sometime later I also moved there to play for Cerro. That's what happens to many Salto players: thanks to baby football, matches on makeshift pitches and street games, they dream of playing in the big leagues for Montevideo, Nacional or Peñarol as a launch pad to Europe or elsewhere abroad.'

As a child Luis loves football more than anything else. His first idols and role models are in his family: his father and his brother Paolo both play. Paolo plays for Club Atlético Basáñez in the Uruguayan second amateur division. Luis copies his brother's movements and gestures, and in return Paolo patiently teaches him the tricks of the trade. He later idolises Brazilian Ronaldo 'O Fenómeno', then River Plate's Fernando Cavenaghi, and then Argentine Gabriel Batitusta, who has played for Newell's, River Plate, Boca Juniors, Fiorentina and Roma.

Once in Montevideo, Luis and his younger brother Maximiliano join Urreta FC, a baby football club in Blanqueada at the crossroads between Arrieta and Pedro Vidal. He is just seven years old. The club is already well established, with plenty of titles and trophies to its name. The coaches watch him try out and decide he can stay. A few days later, 'El Salta' or 'El Salteño' – 'the one from Salto' or 'the little one from Salto', as he becomes known to the coaches and his friends – is put on the bench for a match at Lagomar, a residential area on the coast, about half an hour from the centre of Montevideo. They decide to err on the side of caution as no one has seen him play and they don't know him that well. At the end of the first half, Urreta is down 2-0 and the coach decides to give the new boy a shot. Luis pulls on a number 14 orange checked shirt, similar to Marco van Basten and Ruud Gullit's Dutch team strip in the 1988 European Championship, and heads onto the pitch. And he proceeds to turn the game around with three opportunistic goals. Urreta wins the match and El Salteño gains his team's trust.

'He was an extraordinary kid, with a strong personality. He was afraid of no one,' says Florean Neira, his first coach at Urreta.

By eleven, he catches the eye of someone at

Nacional, and his early dreams look set to become a reality. But not all the technical team are on board – only Wilson Píriz is convinced that inside that clumsy player there is a goal-scoring prodigy. 'He had the virtues, good luck, instinct, innate ability, flukiness, call it what you will. The ball always ended up at his feet and somehow he put it in the back of the net – even blindfolded,' says the former Nacional youth team representative-turned-sports agent.

Initial doubts aside, Luis adapts well at the club. But soon looming adolescence and his parents' divorce seem to affect him, sending him off course. His performance suffers and he seems less interested in training, preferring instead to go out with his friends and consume everything he shouldn't – from pizza and hot dogs to fizzy drinks. He is relegated to the bench and his place on the team is in jeopardy.

'I told him that if he didn't do as he was told, if he wasn't on his best behaviour, he had to go,' says Píriz. 'It was time to sort his life out, from both a sporting and a personal perspective. He had to work hard to move up through the ranks and make it as a professional. He got the gist of what I was saying and made the most of that second chance. Today he is one of the best in the world.'

Following that conversation his performance improves dramatically. He earns back his place in the starting line-up and becomes the top goal-scorer of the '87 team. In one match, against Huracán de Paso la Arena, he scores no fewer than eleven times. 'His initial progress with Nacional was difficult. We would win, but because Luis was transfixed with this desire to win, he would miss easy chances and the crowd would boo him,' says fellow Uruguayan Rubén Sosa, ex-forward at clubs such as Lazio, Inter Milan and Borussia Dortmund, and one of Luis's first coaches. 'They would shout insults at him. Luis didn't care though – he just wanted to be a good footballer.'

* * *

Of the three players, the one who perfectly articulates his passion for the ball is Neymar: 'The football is like the most jealous woman in the world. If you don't treat her well, she will not love you and she can even hurt you. I love her to bits.' And he has proven it ever since he was little. His mother Nadine recalls how her son used to fall asleep hugging his football, and over the years accumulated 54 balls in his room. Little Neymar did not stop playing football for a moment: he played at home, at school, on the beach with his father when he had a spare moment, and on the street with his friends. In Jardim Glória, many remember Juninho as a shy boy who didn't speak much and loved to collect toy cars. He plays on the street, kicking the ball against his neighbours' gates, and practises at the Gremio Praia Grande pitch or on the amazing grass pitch his father has set up in their backyard.

In 2001 he joins Gremetal, already under the guidance of Betinho by this point. 'He was nine at the time. He was a smart kid, lively, always happy,' says Alcides Magri Júnior, one of the club's coaches. 'I remember his smile and the fact that he was great friends with his teammates. He was a great player and had great skills. When he was on the pitch he changed. Nothing got in his way. He was able to turn a match around on his own. But he did not want to be treated differently to the others. He liked being in the group.' Young Neymar's progress quickly exceeds all expectations, and he is soon playing with kids a year or two older than him. He never tires of playing – when training is over he always stays out there kicking the ball around on his own.

'He was polite, respectful towards the teachers and sociable with his classmates. He never missed lessons and never gave us any trouble,' says Maria Antonia Julião Faracco, coordinator at Liceu São Paulo, the private school that invited Neymar to attend on a scholarship. 'We could see he was mad about football. It was immediately obvious. He was always game for a match with his classmates. At break time, students were not allowed to play football but he always found a way around it. He would go to the headmaster and beg him to lend him a football so that he could take some shots or practise keepy-uppy.' The reason for the scholarship is that the school is keen to improve its indoor football team. Neymar – who is playing for Portuguesa at the time – is the boost they are looking for. He is a rising star, and before long the papers are printing photos and articles about him. By thirteen he is already famous locally.

'That was a proper team, that one,' recalls Reginaldo Ferreira de Oliveira, aka Fino, the Portuguesa coach and indoor football coordinator at the school. 'There was Neymar, Dudu, Gustavo and Léo Baptistão. Neymar loved playing football and always wanted to be the best. The best on the street, the best in the district, the best in the city, then the state, then the country and now the best in the world. He always wants more, every single day, and you could see this in him right from when he was a little boy.' Baptistão, who is now a striker for Madrid team Rayo Vallecano, particularly remembers the kid from Mogi das Cruzes standing out above the rest: 'He was the best player on the team. He did incredible things with the ball: dribbling, one-two passes, left- and right-footed lobs. He was smart – he did things way above his age. Everyone knew he would become a star. If the expectations for me or for others like Dudu or Gustavo were average – becoming a professional foot-baller was a distant dream for us – Neymar's future as a star was clear.'

Before long, word of his potential reaches the Peixe (the 'fish', as Santos are known). Towards the end of 2003, former Peixe legend and now manager José Ely de Miranda – known as Zito – decides to go and see him play. He knows straight away that he is witnessing something exceptional. 'I must admit, Neymar filled me with joy,' he recalls. 'He was only eleven years old but he did the same things then as he does today. With the ball at his feet he was incredible, sensational. He was miles above the rest. A real superstar. I went back to Vila Belmiro and spoke to the Santos chairman, Marcelo Teixeira. I told him that we had to get Neymar straight away before someone else snatched him up.' And so, a few months later on 10 May 2004, Neymar da Silva Santos Júnior signs his first contract with Santos, for a five-year term and a salary of 450 Brazilian reais a month (around £110). His career is just beginning.

Chapter 3

Family

Mogi das Cruzes is a municipality of Alto Tietê, a region to the east of the metropolitan area of São Paulo in Brazil. It's where Neymar da Silva Santos used to play football and where his son, Neymar Júnior, is born.

Father and son share the same profession. In 1989, at the age of 24, Neymar Pai joins União Mogi, a modest club founded at the beginning of the 20th century. 'He was a good forward, a number 7. He played on the wing. He was quick, skilful, good at dribbling and always targeted his opponent. He was a cheerful chap, outgoing, a nice person, easy to get on with,' says Carlos 'Pintado' Juvêncio. The club's sporting director also remembers little Ney: 'Pai brought him to training. He was the team mascot.' He recalls how both father and son had the same touch and ability to dribble – although Juninho was quicker, lighter on his feet, more creative. Ex-Brazil goalkeeper Waldir Peres, who played in the Spain World Cup in 1982 and was União coach in 1993 and 1995, agrees. 'Neymar Júnior is a better dribbler. He always goes for the finish and looks to score goals.'

But let's backtrack a moment to an important anecdote. In 1991, at the age of 26, in the church of São Pedro 'O Pescador' in São Vicente, Neymar da Silva Santos marries Nadine Gonçalves. They had met when she was sixteen and he was eighteen and a rising star at Portuguesa Santista. Their first son is born at 2.15am on 5 February 1992, a natural birth with no complications, both mother and son are fine. The baby weighs 3.78kg, around 8lb 5oz. Nadine and Neymar Pai are delighted to welcome Neymar Júnior. 'He turned up at the hotel where the club was staying in a euphoric state,' recalls Waldir Peres. 'He swore that one day his son would be the best Brazilian football player in history.'

Their happiness is almost cut short one Sunday in June 1992 while driving to São Vicente to visit family. It's a rainy day and the roads are wet. Suddenly a car on the opposite side of the road tries to overtake and cut into the oncoming traffic. Neymar Pai swerves and tries to accelerate out of the way but he is in fifth gear and the impact is unavoidable.

The couple look behind them and Juninho is not there. They think he has been thrown out of the car on impact and fear they have lost him forever. A couple of cars stop to help and Juninho is found underneath the seat, covered in blood. His parents had been beside themselves with panic. An ambulance takes them to the nearest hospital. Nadine escapes with just a few scratches. Juninho needs a larger bandage – the blood had come from a small cut on his head, caused by a piece of flying glass. Neymar Pai is not so lucky: he has a dislocated pelvis and has to have emergency surgery. He is unable to play for almost a year and has to undergo treatment, rehabilitation and physiotherapy.

Neymar Pai's career is irreparably damaged by the accident. Although he makes it back onto the pitch, he will never play at the same level again. From then until his retirement in 1997 he plays for a handful of small teams and eventually wins the Matto-Grossense league, the only title of his career, just as he is about to hang up his boots.

At 32, it is time for Neymar Pai to make a fresh start, and decides to move his wife and two children – little Rafaella had been born the previous March – to Jardim Glória in Praia Grande. They live at 374 Rua B: a pastel green, low-rise house at the end of the street, built by Neymar Pai on a twelve-by-30-metre plot of land. It has a corrugated iron roof and a large patio. He bought the land using what was left of the savings earned during his footballing career. 'I am not a daddy's boy. I grew up in a *favela*. My family was humble. We had serious financial problems,' his son will comment years later. Nadine works as a cook and Pai as a mechanic, a bricklayer, a foreman … until eventually he decides to dedicate himself completely to managing his son's unstoppable career. Despite their hardships, he has always been there for Ney and has given him as much support as possible.

'They treated him with great affection and love. Even if the family's finances were not the best, they always did what they could for their son. They educated him to be honest, sincere – you know, a good boy,' says Betinho. Neymar Pai is Juninho's most trusted advisor. He accompanies him on his first trip to Spain, when he is barely fourteen, for a trial at Real Madrid.

Pai manages his son's finances, but he is also the one who advises him to step up when he finds out that he is to become a father. Little David Lucca is born on 24 August 2011 at the São Luiz hospital in São Paulo. The footballer's on-off relationship with the baby's mother, Carolina Dantas, hasn't lasted, but they are on good terms. 'Juninho is a marvellous, caring, doting father and a friend who has stood by me,' says the young mother, who is studying medicine. 'When he was at Santos, he would come and see him as often as he could, he was caring and showered him with gifts. Sometimes he stayed the night to spend time with David.' In keeping with his deeply held religious beliefs, Neymar has his son baptised at the Peniel Baptist Church.

Unlike teammates Suárez and Messi, Juninho is yet to find his soulmate. But he has certainly enjoyed serious romances with some high-profile girls – most notably with Brazilian actress Bruna Marquezine, in a relationship known for break-ups, reconciliations and rumours. Not much is known about his private life in Barcelona, just that his father is there with him, while his mother has stayed in Brazil with Rafaella and visits once a month. In any case, he has no time to be lonely, as he is always spending time with some childhood friend or other – or at least, that's what it looks like judging by his social networking pages.

* * *

Leo Messi has also maintained very close ties with his homeland, Argentina, despite having spent half his life in Barcelona. Ever since he arrived he has always been surrounded and supported by his loved ones, notably his father Jorge and brother Rodrigo. But in recent years one person in particular has become his rock: Antonella Rocuzzo, his wife and the mother of his son Thiago, born on 2 November 2012. They have known each other since they were five: she is the first cousin of Leo's childhood friend Lucas Scaglia. 'I have seen her grow up and she has seen me grow up. Our families know each other, so I didn't have any doubts,' the Barça number 10 has said. Antonella is the same age as the Flea and is also a Newell's fan. She studied dentistry and then communications before going to live in Barcelona with Leo.

They are both from Rosario, the largest city in the Argentine state of Santa Fe, on the banks of the Paraná river. It is a city of the grandchildren of immigrants – like Leo's family, who have Italian and Spanish ancestors. Back in Rosario, Jorge was the head of department at steel manufacturer Acindar, in Villa Constitución, some 50 kilometres outside Rosario, while his mother Celia Cuccittini worked in a magnet manufacturing workshop. They met as youngsters, fell in love and got engaged.

They are married on 17 June 1978 at the Corazón de María church. The country is fully absorbed in the World Cup, which host nation Argentina wins a few days later – a triumph which seems to momentarily banish the horrors of General Jorge Rafael Videla's dictatorship.

Their first two sons are born during a period of military rule. But Lionel, their third, arrives during the early years of democracy. It's a difficult time, and the country is on the verge of civil war.

On 23 June 1987 Celia is admitted to the Garibaldi hospital. The pregnancy has been uneventful, but during the final few hours complications arise. Gynaecologist Norberto Odetto diagnoses severe foetal distress and decides to induce labour in order to avoid any lasting effects on the baby. A few minutes before six in the morning, Lionel Andrés Messi is born, weighing three kilos and measuring 47 centimetres in length, as red as a tomato and with one ear completely folded over due to the force of labour – anomalies which, as with many other newborns, disappear within the first few hours. After the scare comes happiness: the new arrival is a little bit pink, but healthy.

Once they are discharged, Celia and baby Lionel come home to the house that Jorge built over many weekends with the help of his father Eusebio, on a 300-square-metre plot of family-owned land. It's a two-storey brick building with a backyard where the children can play, in Las Heras, a neighbourhood of humble, hardworking people in the southern part of Rosario. Six months later, Lionel can be seen in a family album, chubby-cheeked and smiling, on his parents' bed, dressed in little blue trousers and a white T-shirt.

The years pass, and Leo grows up kicking a ball around, just like the other kids in his neighbourhood. He stands out because of his abilities, but he is also extremely shy and much smaller than others his age. At nine and a half his parents take him to see Doctor Diego Schwarzstein, and discover that Leo has a growth hormone deficit. Over the next two years, Jorge's medical insurance pays for the treatment, but when they will no longer cover it, he goes to Newell's for help. He is aware of his son's potential, and is convinced that football will be the answer to Leo's height problem.

Gradually Jorge Messi begins to get involved in managing Leo's career, until eventually he becomes his agent, negotiating his contracts and publicity deals. Nothing is agreed without his blessing. He lives with the Flea during the early years at Barcelona, where Leo begins to mature as a footballer – and continues his treatment.

Meanwhile Celia, brother Matías and little sister María Sol find it more difficult to adapt to life in the Catalan capital, preferring instead to return to Rosario. But despite the distance, they remain extremely close as a family, and the Blaugrana number 10 returns home to be with them whenever he can. In terms of his private life, Leo Messi keeps a low profile.

* * *

Luis Suárez also leads a fairly quiet life with his wife Sofia Balbi and their two children. He comes from humble beginnings, but unlike Neymar and Messi he comes from a broken home.

He is born on 24 January 1987 in the Salto hospital, the fourth son of Sandra and Rodolfo. His older siblings are Paolo, Giovanna and Leticia, and his younger siblings are Maximiliano and Diego. He is a skinny kid with a full head of dark hair, a healthy kid who, unlike his brothers and sisters, doesn't even get the dreaded chickenpox. But at two years of age he

gives his parents a scare when he gets appendicitis, followed by peritonitis two days after surgery. The pain is
unbearable and little Suárez cannot even stand up. It
is an unforeseen complication after a routine operation, and the doctors have to reopen the wound to sort
it out. Slowly but surely the intestinal infection heals
and he recovers.

The family lives near the General de Artigas army
barracks. Luis's father, like his father before him, is in
the military, and plays in his regiment's football team.
He's a good defender who plays on the right. It's not
easy getting past him – he's a tough nut who can be
quick-witted and crafty depending on the situation: a
quality Luis seems to have inherited.

In 1994 Rodolfo asks to be transferred to the
Uruguayan capital, Montevideo. Luis does not want
to leave Salto and no one can convince him – so much
so that he ends up staying with his grandmother for
a month before rejoining his family. After moving to
the capital, however, he would only return to Salto on
the odd occasion.

The Suárez Díaz family settle in La Blanqueada
neighbourhood, where the locals are football mad.
But the move from the hinterland to the big city has
not been without its complications for the kids, who
have had to leave all their grandparents, uncles, aunts,
relatives and childhood friends. They have been used
to playing on the streets from morning to night, which

they can no longer do. And the city kids make fun of their accent, their old trainers and their dated clothes.

As Suárez has admitted on several occasions: 'We were a lower class family – and a big family – so we could not afford certain treats. I never asked my parents to buy me the pair of football boots I so longed for. My parents did all they could and I am very grateful to them but they could not provide for us as they wanted to, just the bare minimum.'

Luis's father leaves the army and finds a job in El Trigal biscuit factory, while Sandra works as a cleaner. Luis attends school number 171 with his brothers. He enjoys maths and gets on with his homework at home. Who knows, if he hadn't been a footballer maybe he could have been a good accountant.

In 1996, when Maxi is eight and Luis is nine, Rodolfo and Sandra get divorced. Rodolfo leaves his job at the biscuit factory and moves to Carrasco in another part of the city, where he finds a job as a porter at Club Biguá de Villa Biarritz basketball club. His sons rarely see him but they keep in touch. 'My dad was an alcoholic,' Maximiliano will tell French sport magazine *So Foot* several years later. 'He would go to the stadium when we were playing and shout and talk randomly to people. It was embarrassing. It was the same at home. The arguing was constant between my mum and my dad.'

Sandra has to find additional work in order to

provide for her children. But it is hard to make ends meet. 'We lived in a single five-by-three-metre room. For months on end, we ate the same thing: sausages and rice.'

It's a difficult time for Luis, and he only manages to find his way after meeting the girl who is to be the love of his life. She is twelve and he is fifteen. They meet for the first time at Fabric, a nightclub in Montevideo which puts on a matinee for kids, and they start going out. Sofia Balbi, the girl in question, starts turning up to Luis's training sessions and the Nacional youth matches, and Luis's closest friends know that he is madly in love. Sofia might be young but she is mature and down to earth, and she is to become the support system that Luis has been lacking. Her help and support are incredibly important for his soul and help him keep his feet on the ground.

All is well until the day she drops a bombshell: she is leaving for Europe. It is October 2004. Her family have been hit hard by the financial crisis in Uruguay which has crippled the middle class, and they have decided to move to Barcelona. Luis is distraught, but they decide to maintain a long-distance relationship. He begins to work hard, as he has realised that football could become his future, his livelihood, and that perhaps one day it could help him reunite with his love.

Luis and Sofia are apart for nearly two years. Then the Nacional number 9 receives an offer from

Dutch club FC Groningen. It's not Spain, but at least Groningen is closer to Barcelona. Suárez accepts the offer. 'If Sofia had been in Uruguay, I may not have made the decision I made,' he will later admit. He flies to Europe to sign the contract, and the club give him twelve days off. He is on the next plane to Barcelona.

And nothing can come between them. In March 2009 Sofia and Luis tie the knot in a small civil ceremony. And on 26 December they have a church wedding back in Montevideo, followed by a big party for 500 guests. On 5 August 2010 in Barcelona their daughter Delfina is born, followed three years later by Benjamin. Their love story has already spanned twelve years – twelve incredible years in the life and career of Luis Suárez. Without Sofia's presence and support, perhaps he would not be where he is today. She knows him better than anyone, his obsessions and his flaws, she knows how to keep him on the straight and narrow, while offering him the stability he needs. She is not the typical WAG who wants to be in the limelight or on the front of every gossip magazine. She is a life companion, a partner, his support when the going gets tough. She is at his side following sendings-off and ear-biting incidents. She is there for him when he is banned from the pitch.

Chapter 4

Clubs

Messi, Neymar and Suárez: three footballing icons, three players with very different career trajectories. Though they wear the same kit, they have had very different journeys to Barcelona.

For Leo, Barça is his home, where he has grown up as a person and as a professional. In Neymar's case, it's not his first club, but it is his first European team. And for Luis, it's the pinnacle of a career forged step by step at some of the best known clubs on the continent. Let's look back at their journeys ...

* * *

At thirteen years of age, Leo is already a well-known figure in Rosario youth football. He is playing in the minor leagues for Newell's, the team of his dreams. The newspapers dedicate double-page spreads to him, and word of his talents has even reached Buenos Aires. One fine day in 2000 the Messi family receive a visit from Martín Montero and Fabián Soldini of Marka sports agency. They want to represent the young

player and they want to float the possibility of trying
their luck with Barcelona. Nowadays, the Messis do
not speak of these particular agents, who, it is claimed,
did not actually help their son.

Regardless, a few months later, on 17 September,
the Flea and his father touch down at El Prat airport
in Barcelona.

It seems strange that an entire family should put
all their faith in a thirteen-year-old boy. Before they
got married, Celia and Jorge had already thought of
emigrating to Australia – they wanted a new life in a
new world. Things were not bad, but they knew they
could not achieve much more. Their life in Argentina
could not change for the better. They were looking for
a new opportunity for their children, and Leo could
receive his medical treatment in Barcelona and continue to improve his football at a great club, as his
talent deserved. But it was not an easy decision. The
Messis asked themselves time and again whether or
not they were doing the right thing. Before leaving,
they gathered the family around the table and asked
each one of them what they wanted to do, making it
clear that if even one of them did not want to go, they
would all stay in Rosario.

During the course of a week, Leo trains and plays
a short match with children his age. Jorge watches in
silence from the stands, just as he always used to do
at the Rosario grounds. All the coaches who see him

comment that the Argentine kid plays very well, but it is Carles 'Charly' Rexach, then Barcelona's technical director, who must make the decision regarding his future. The matter has been left up in the air and needs to be resolved as soon as possible, so a match is organised between cadets, aged fourteen–fifteen, and first-year students at the Miniestadi third ground on Tuesday 3 October at 5.00pm. Charly wants to see how Leo fares against older lads.

'What had I seen? A kid who was very small, but different, with incredible self-confidence, agile, fast, technically polished, who could run flat out with the ball, and who was capable of swerving round whoever stood in his way. It wasn't difficult to spot it. His talents, which are now known to everyone, were more noticeable at thirteen. There are footballers who need a team in order to shine – not him. To those who tell me that I was the one who discovered Messi, I always reply: if a Martian had seen him play they would have realised that he was very special,' recalls Charly.

The boss has agreed, and the deal is done. Two days later, Leo and his father are on a flight to Buenos Aires. They return home happy. But in the end, things do not go as smoothly as planned. Rexach has not forgotten the obstacles he encountered in trying to convince the club that Messi was worth the effort: 'First of all, he was foreign, and the law doesn't allow a foreign child to play in any national league. A considerable handicap. Second, he was a kid. He could end up not becoming a Barcelona player, whether due to his own choice, injury, or age. Third, what are his parents going to do? We'd have to find work for them if they moved to Spain. And finally, the boy has a growth problem, he needs treatment. '

He is in no doubt, but some of the Barça staff just see Leo as a small, scrawny kid. Time ticks by, and Leo's agents threaten to offer him to Real. Finally, on 8 January 2011 they reach a firm agreement. Two letters are written to Jorge Messi: one from Charly, who confirms the sporting agreement made with the family in Barcelona, and the other from Joan Lacueva, then director of professional football, regarding the financial terms. In it he includes details of the house they are to rent, the school, and the 7 million pesetas (around £40,000) Jorge would receive as remuneration for a position at the club, which is as good a way as any of remunerating the footballer himself, who would only have been entitled to a study grant. The letter is enough to convince the Messis to pack their bags. On 15 February 2001, in the depths of the Barcelona winter, the entire family touches down at the Catalan airport.

The photo on his first Barcelona ID badge shows him with a round face and a quiff. And a smile – that was soon to disappear because during the first few months of his new life on Catalan soil, things do not go very well for Leo. He is a foreigner and cannot play in any national competitions, which means he cannot join the children's A team, which should be his team: instead he has to make do with the children's B team, which plays in the Catalan regional league. And another thing: Newell's is not willing to make the necessary transfer arrangements so that Barcelona can enrol him in the Spanish Football Federation. And that's not all – there is worse still to come. On 21 April a Tortosa defender tackles him hard: the result is a fractured left leg. It is the first injury in Leo's career. First he needs a splint, then a plaster cast and finally rehab – he won't be able to play again until 6 June.

By the end of the season, Leo has only played in two official matches and one friendly tournament. Meanwhile, his family has had difficulty adapting to life in the Catalan capital. During the Spanish summer vacation, when they are all back in Rosario, the family weigh up their options and reach some decisions. Jorge and Celia (who has had to return early to be with her sister, who has undergone an operation) decide that María Sol and the boys should stay in Argentina. They ask Leo what he wants to do. Does he want to return to Barcelona or go back to his old life in Rosario? The boy has no doubt in his mind. He makes it clear that he wants to succeed in Barcelona, there is no need to worry about him. And so, only five months after their arrival, the family is forced to divide in two. On one side of the ocean, Celia, María Sol, Matías and Rodrigo; on the other, Jorge and Leo.

Finally the FIFA documents arrive, allowing the Spanish FA to arrange Leo's signing. And on 17 February 2002, almost a year after his arrival in Barcelona, Leo is permitted to enter the championship. He plays against Esplugues de Llobregat at the Can Vidalet ground. He only comes on after half-time, but adds three gems to the final scoreline of 1-14. Little more than a month later, on 29 March, he wins his first Barça title. With much elation, they win the league thanks to a 6-0 victory over El Prat. The bad days are over.

16 November 2003 is a date that will forever be etched on Leo Messi's mind. He is sixteen years, four months and 23 days old and today he makes his debut with the first team against Porto, to celebrate the inauguration of the Portuguese club's new Dragão Stadium. For once, the match is perhaps of lesser importance. A bit of football, very few emotions, a decidedly boring fixture, which, in keeping with the script and to the delight of the home team, ends with a 2-0 victory to Porto.

Lionel Messi debuts in the 74th minute. He is the third substitution for Barcelona, invited to take his place as one of the protagonists of this Portuguese fiesta. This Barcelona team has been obliged to look to youth team players to fill the teamsheet.

The internationals have been called up to their respective countries, occupied elsewhere in the Euro 2004 qualifying rounds or friendlies.

Leo replaces Fernando Navarro. He is wearing number 14. And he cannot wait to show what he is worth. So much so that he makes himself noticed in the fifteen minutes he is on the pitch by creating two scoring chances. At the final whistle, Barça coach Frank Rijkaard comments that 'he is a boy with a lot of talent and a promising future'.

*   *   *

Neymar Júnior knows all about the challenge of living up to expectations. And he does just that on Saturday 7 March 2009 in his debut with the Peixe first team at the Pacaembu, the São Paulo municipal stadium. Santos are playing Oeste from Itápolis in a Paulista league match. The 22,000 paying supporters are mostly Peixe fans.

Kick-off is at 6.30pm and the fans immediately begin chanting for Neymar to be sent into battle. Vágner Mancini, the coach who took over the team on 14 February following Márcio Fernández's resignation, resists until thirteen minutes into the second half. He whispers a final few instructions and, two minutes later, sends him on in place of Colombian midfielder Mauricio Molina. Neymar strides onto the pitch wearing the number 18 black and white shirt, as the stadium fills with a huge roar. It is the moment Juninho and the fans have been waiting for.

Neymar dribbles around one player to the right of the area, then unleashes a powerful shot that hits the crossbar and the post, narrowly missing the goal. It is his first touch, and it could scarcely have been a better start for the boy from Mogi das Cruzes. At the end of the match (2-1 to Santos), the number 18 jogs off the pitch to a round of applause, and heads off to play football with his friends. He has made his first appearance and has helped the team, who had been unable to break the deadlock in the first half, to a victory. He has not let anyone down.

Eight days later he scores his first goal, once again at the Pacaembu, this time against Paulista FC. The play starts in the Peixe's own half. Molina pushes past the halfway line and passes to Germano, who spots an opening on the left and passes to Triguinho, who in turn darts into the area and crosses it into the centre. Neymar bursts forward from nowhere and scores his first goal with a diving header. It is 6.37pm and Santos are 3-0 up. Neymar celebrates by pointing to the sky, jumping and punching the air, mimicking his hero, Pelé. At the end of the match he explains: 'I wanted to celebrate that way because I had promised my father I would do so.' He dedicates the goal to Ilzemar, his paternal grandfather, who was a huge fan of Pelé and who had shown his grandson so many videos of O Rei's goals. He used to take him to the park and kicked the ball around with Juninho while his cousins played with their dolls. Ilzemar died in 2008 without having seen his grandson play for the Peixe. The dedication is a tribute to the memory of his grandfather and a way to please his father.

But as time goes on, Ney is forced to wait patiently for more opportunities. In July 2009, Vanderlei Luxemburgo replaces Mancini as the Peixe coach, and he is not fully convinced about the kid's abilities. He keeps him on the bench for almost every match and insists he go on a high-calorie diet. 'He's like a stick insect. He's little and can't withstand the physical contact of a match,' asserts the new boss. 'He looks like Robinho when he started. He needs to build up his muscle mass. I don't want to burn him out.' It's a difficult time for Juninho, but all that changes with the arrival of Dorival Silvestre Júnior. On 30 December 2009, at his presentation as the new Santos coach, he acknowledges that he is taking on a group of young players developed by the club, who can be trusted. Neymar is one of them. He can now put the stick insect nickname behind him and enjoy being back in the thick of it.

Santos and the kid from Mogi are on top form, as they demonstrate on 10 March 2010 when they beat Naviraiense 10-0. It is the best haul in the history of both the Santos team and the Copa do Brasil. Neymar scores the second and the seventh – the latter a particularly memorable moment in the 54th minute. He receives the ball from Giovanni on the edge of the box. He bypasses one, two, three defenders with a series of feints, and the goalkeeper doesn't stand a chance. The TV commentators shout 'Gol de Placa!' – an expression alluding to Pelé's great goal on 5 March 1961 against Fluminense, for which a commemorative plaque was put up at the Maracanã stadium.

But it is not the avalanche of goals or stunning performances that are winning over the fans – it is the spreading of joy and the desire to have fun. Each goal is celebrated with a new jig, something fun and different. In a match against Guaraní, the players invent one dance after another: the baseball hat and rap, the tennis match, the motorbike, the lorry, the rolling planes, the merry-go-round, the military march, the shoe-shiner and the signature dances to music from the movies. The range of celebrations is seemingly endless.

Santos go on to win two league titles in the season: the first and second of Neymar's career. First they triumph in the Paulista championship, and then they clinch the Copa do Brazil. Neymar is the highest goalscorer of the tournament with eleven, and the country's newest idol.

But a few short weeks later he will fall from grace. On 15 September Santos are playing Atlético

Goianiense at their home ground, Vila Belmiro. Five minutes before the final whistle the number 11 goes down in the box – penalty. He collects the ball and is preparing to place it on the spot when Léo, the Santos number 3, comes over to tell him the coach has decided that Marcel should take the shot. Neymar lets the ball drop, holds out his arms and turns to the dugout, unleashing some choice words in the direction of coach Dorival Júnior. Léo goes over to Neymar, puts his arm around him and tries to calm him down. Even Marquinos, who had been on the touchline, goes over to try to placate him, but Neymar shrugs him off and heads towards the centre of the pitch with a bottle of water in his hand. He has a go at Roberto Brun and Edu Dracena, the team captain, who tries to calm him down. Marcel converts the penalty to make it 4-2 to Santos, but Neymar doesn't care, he is still having a strop.

After the match, Goianiense coach René Simões vents his annoyance: 'I am deeply disappointed today. I have spent my entire life in football but I have hardly ever seen someone as rude – from a sporting perspective – as this boy, Neymar. I have always worked with young players and I have never seen anything like it. What he did was unacceptable. Even the Santos players did not agree with his behaviour. It is time someone educated him or we will create a monster.' The Brazilian press is full of talk about bad boy antics, saying the fame has gone to his head and that he has no respect. The player apologises on social media, but it is not enough. Years later he will recall that fateful 15 September as one of the worst days of his life. The coach decides to make an example of him, fining him 50,000 reais (around £12,500) and taking him off the team for the next two matches. But rumour has it that the ban angers club president Luis Álvaro de Oliveira Ribeiro, who considers it excessive. A few hours later, it emerges that Dorival Júnior will be leaving his post as manager. Neymar has learned the hard way.

By contrast, 2011 is a stellar year, full of momentous occasions for Neymar, as he becomes a father and is hailed as one of the best footballers of his time. On 22 June, Santos is at home to Uruguayan team Peñarol in the final of the Copa Libertadores. The Peixe are in a creative mood and have plenty of chances but are unable to get anything through in the first half. Shortly after half-time, though, Neymar opens up the game with the first goal: Arouca carves out a lovely little manoeuvre from the midfield and finds the number 11 free on the left, who smacks the ball on the volley past the goalkeeper into the right corner of the net. Goaaaaal! The players are ecstatic as it is clear the title is theirs for the taking. Danilo drives home the second and it looks to be all over. But there is still time for a comeback. In the 79th minute, while trying to clear his area, Santos defender Durval scores an own goal. The fans cannot believe their eyes, and some turn their backs, unable to watch. They only turn around again when Argentine referee Sergio Pezzotta blows the final whistle. The Peixe have won the most prestigious Latin American title for the third time in their history.

Just a month later, on 27 July, Ney comes face to face with Ronaldinho's Flamengo at the Vila Belmiro. The 'Gaucho' scores three goals and gives his best performance since leaving Barcelona. Meanwhile Ney scores two – the first of which is a masterpiece that will later win him the FIFA Puskás Award for the 2011 goal of the year. Unsurprisingly, his contract with the Peixe is renewed on 9 November. The only disappointment of the year is losing the Club World Cup to Barcelona.

In the months that follow, Ney enters the hall of fame of the greatest goal-scorers in Santos's history. Thanks to his efforts, the team can celebrate their centenary year as Paulista champions for the third year in a row. And Neymar is named by Uruguayan newspaper *El País* as the South American Footballer of the Year for the second year running.

The press and the fans are already predicting that he won't be staying long at Santos. The prospect of him signing for a European club has become a matter of national interest. His every movement is under scrutiny and he is accused of being distracted and of losing his rhythm on the pitch. He is finding it difficult to score goals.

On 26 May 2013 he plays his final match with the Peixe. Nine years after arriving at Santos, five years after his debut in the famous white shirt, 299 appearances, 138 goals and six titles later (three Paulistãos, one Copa do Brasil, one Libertadores and one Recopa Sudamericana), Neymar da Silva Santos Júnior bids farewell to the club where he has grown up. Next stop: Barcelona.

* * *

Like Neymar, Luis Suárez also makes his first team debut with his childhood club: Nacional de Montevideo. His first match is on 3 May 2005 in the second round of the Copa Libertadores. They are playing Júnior FC at the Colombian team's stadium in Barraquilla, and it is sweltering. The Uruguayans are knocked out after a 3-2 defeat, and Lucho only plays for fifteen minutes. But it's ample time to show coach Martín Lasarte his skills.

Nonetheless, over the next few months, he has to content himself with playing a few minutes here and there, the tail ends of matches. Finally, on 22 October he is in the starting line-up against River Plate, playing as a centre forward in the number 9 shirt. He plays well but he doesn't score. It's a pattern for the next five matches – superb performances but no goals.

As centre forward he should be getting into the box, turning and shooting or heading, but he would get the ball 40 metres out, dodge past two or three defenders and then mess it up when he got to the opponents' goal. The crowd are not behind him: they begin to boo and tease him every time he touches the ball.

Then comes the match against Defensor on 4 December 2005. Luis is on the right, running rings around the defence. The opposition needs to find a solution and improvise to stop the Suárez onslaught. They try their best but there is nothing they can do. On the stroke of the 60th minute, Suárez scores an incredible goal: Alberto Silva releases the ball to the edge of the area where Luis is waiting with his back to goal. He controls the ball with his left foot, loses a defender who had been stuck to him like glue and unleashes a shot at waist height that completely evades goalkeeper Juan Guillermo Castillo. The match ends 2-2, but it is Suárez's coming of age, and a big relief for Lasarte. The little guy has more than convinced those who matter that he is worthy. It's a definite turning point. From now on, no one dares to challenge his authority or boo him.

Nacional ends the season winning the Uruguayan championship for the second year running. And a new star has been born: Suárez has scored twelve goals in 28 matches, just one fewer than Chori Castro who played 34.

He has just begun to shine, and he is on the way up. On 11 July 2006 he is presented as the newest signing at FC Groningen, the Dutch team founded in 1971 that has yet to win a single national or international title, and which floats in the middle of the Eredivisie, the country's highest league. After signing his contract, he is photographed shaking hands with sporting director Hans Nijland. The picture shows him in a black suit and white shirt, hair gelled with little waves in it, flashing a toothy smile.

He doesn't have an easy time at first. He is overweight, and the club nutritionist puts him on a diet. Fiancée Sofia is asked to ensure he stays away from the pizza and fizzy drinks – just water, water and more water. In addition, he finds it tough adapting to the training sessions, which are much more strict than in Uruguay. His teammates think it's strange that he carries a thermos of hot water wherever he goes so that he can sip his traditional *mate* tea in the changing room. They also don't like the way he argues with the ref, fakes falling down and talks and shouts constantly while on the pitch.

In his first match he only gets to play a few minutes with the first team. Communication is a struggle, Luis feels misunderstood and coach Ron Jans loses his patience with him. Luis isn't playing how he wanted him to play and he is arguing with anyone and everyone. When he begins to gesticulate at the bench it's the last straw for the coach, who brings him off. Luis leaves the pitch without even shaking hands with his teammates and heads for the showers. It is raining and the coach is so angry he throws an umbrella at him.

But the next Sunday he will find himself lending Luis the umbrella and making him do a lap of honour in front of thousands of enthusiastic fans. It is to be a miracle of a match, as Luis and Sofia will later call it. The game in question is on 1 October 2006, the sixth matchday of the season, and Groningen are at home to Vitesse. Suárez is wearing number 9 and is in the starting line-up. A minute before the final whistle his team are losing 2-3. It's at that moment that he finds the ball at his feet and sends it flying into the back of the net for the equaliser. He blows kisses to the crowd and goes to celebrate in front of the stands. But it's not over yet. In the 91st minute he controls the ball after a cross, loses the defender, and slams the ball in once again with a left-footed shot. The stadium erupts with delight and his ecstatic teammates race over to pile themselves on top of him. Groningen have come within a single point of leaders Ajax. Things have finally clicked for Luis, and in a few short months he will become the green and white fans' biggest hero. By the end of the season, Groningen are eighth in the league. Suárez has scored ten goals in 29 matches, three fewer than the top goal-scorer Nevland. He has transformed from street player to stadium player.

An all-round footballer. A *rummelaaetje*, a hustler, as the Dutch would say. Ajax have him in their sights.

The move will be anything but straightforward, with Groningen and Ajax becoming embroiled in a lengthy dispute. But eventually his transfer to the country's biggest title-winners is finalised on 9 August 2007. A week later he makes his debut with Ajax in a Champions League fixture against SK Slavia Prague. The match ends badly, with the Lancers losing 1-0. But Suárez has put on a good performance.

Four months after his arrival, Ajax hires a new coach, Adrie Koster. He and Lucho get on well. Step by step, match by match, the Uruguayan is beginning to fit in with Ajax's style of play and their formation, which rewards team players and focuses on ball possession.

By the end of his first year with the new team he is really getting into his stride, demonstrating his goal-scoring capabilities: seventeen in the league, 22 across all competitions. Unfortunately, the team has to make do with second place. And another thing best forgotten is Luis's argument with teammate Albert Luque, the former Mallorca and Deportivo La Coruña player. They get into a dispute on the pitch during a match against Feyenoord on 11 November 2007 and they end up coming to blows in the changing room. It appears to be over the fact that Luis wouldn't let him take a free kick.

There is yet another change in the dugout in the 2008-09 season, with the arrival of three-time Ballon d'Or winner Marco van Basten. It seems likely that the former striker with 300 goals to his name – nicknamed the Swan of Utrecht due to his role as one of the greatest and most graceful players of all time – would get on with a striker like Suárez. And yet the two do not see eye to eye at all. Their vision of the game is completely different. Van Basten tries to find the most useful position for Luis, but in doing so, moves him around too much. Luis simply doesn't understand the new coach's approach.

Van Basten wants to tame the beast and demands that Suárez reduce the number of fouls he makes. He ends the season with 22 league goals – 34 in total – just one fewer than the Eredivisie top goal-scorer, AZ Alkmaar's Mounir El Hamdaoui. But he is also second on the list of the most cautioned players, with seven yellow cards. The Ajax fans don't care. To them he's an idol, they love him, and vote him Player of the Year. And he earns the nickname El Pistolero after scoring a goal and then miming pulling out two pistols and blowing the smoke off the top. He came up with the celebration after chatting to Sofia and his brother Paolo – it was a popular gesture that had captured the imagination of the fans and journalists.

Lucho certainly has the fans and the hacks in the palm of his hand. Marco van Basten, on the other hand, is on the way out. On 6 May 2009 he submits his letter of resignation because he has not managed to achieve the number of goals set when joining the club. He hasn't won the league or qualified for the Champions League.

As if everything Luis has achieved so far is not enough to confirm his star status at the club, on 15 July 2009 he is named captain. The armband seems to make him more disciplined, just as long as his temper is in check. And it enables him to mature even more as a player. In addition, new coach Martin Jol is allowing him more freedom to move, and Luis responds in the form of goals. In December he is named goalscorer of the year and makes it onto the Eredivisie fantasy eleven. In March 2010 he becomes the top scorer across all European tournaments. Ajax lose the league again, but as a consolation prize they beat Feyenoord 4-1 to clinch the Dutch Cup. It's Suárez's first trophy in Europe, and the icing on the cake of a fabulous season.

When his third season at Ajax begins, things are going smoothly. He is the leader in the changing room and on the pitch ... for better or worse. On Saturday 20 November 2010 Ajax are playing the infamous derby against PSV Eindhoven at the Amsterdam Arena – a match in which emotions always run high. In the 92nd minute there is a scuffle on the pitch. Tempers are flaring, when suddenly Suárez reaches boiling point, throws himself at his opponent and bites him on the neck. Their teammates pull them apart and the two of them mouth off at each other. It is over in a flash but the incident has been caught on camera. As the replay rolls, the Dutch commentator exclaims: 'Yes, Suárez has bitten Bakkal! I have never seen anything like it.'

The next morning, *De Telegraaf* leads with the headline: 'The Cannibal of Ajax'. The newspaper calls on the footballing federation to intervene and take measures against Suárez. Ajax decides to fine Luis and suspend him for two matches. The KNVB disciplinary committee comes down harder with a seven-match ban, to include the two-match ban by the club.

'There are two Luises: the one on the pitch and the one off the pitch. Off the pitch, he is a quiet, reserved, pleasant guy. You just have to watch him when he is with Sofia or Delfina to realise what he is really like. On the pitch he morphs into someone who is nervous, tense, stressed and angry. It is as though these two people co-exist: Dr Jekyll and Mr Hyde. Why? Because he lives football with an intense passion. He always wants to win, come what may,' explains Herman Pinkster, the Ajax staff member closest to Suárez during his three and a half years at the club.

Luis apologises in Dutch and Spanish to Bakkal and Ajax via a Facebook video posted on 2 December 2010: 'I made a mistake, but in that moment I was pumped, my heart rate was racing and sometimes you do not think before acting. I regret what I did, I am my worst critic. I know I normally do not react like this. Now I just want to get back to working hard for the team.'

But his days with the Lancers are numbered. On 28 January 2011, three days before the end of the winter transfer window, Luis becomes a Liverpool player. Four months later, Ajax win the league after a six-year drought.

On 2 February Luis makes his Anfield debut wearing number 7 against Stoke City. He comes on in the 63rd minute, and scores within fifteen minutes.

However, his numbers in that initial half-season are not great and he aspires to bigger things. But the new season gets off to a bad start. On 15 October 2011 Man United left-back Patrice Evra accuses Luis of racially abusing him and calling him 'black'. The Uruguayan denies it, but the case whips up so much controversy that the British government decides to stage a special racism summit with various football authorities in an attempt to prevent any similar behaviour occurring again on the pitch. Meanwhile Suárez receives an eight-match ban and is fined £40,000.

Fortunately for both Luis and Liverpool, the media eventually turns its attention back to football. On 26 February 2012, with Luis back on the pitch, Liverpool face Cardiff in the Carling Cup at Wembley

Stadium and it's 2-2 after extra time. The Reds win on penalties to take home their first title in six years. By the end of the season, Suárez has notched up seventeen goals in 39 matches, notwithstanding the eight-match ban. He is also the club's top scorer with eleven Premier League goals.

The 2012-13 season progresses well, and El Pistolero is enjoying himself. He is seeing eye to eye with coach Brendan Rogers and is on board with his attacking style. By 20 April he has scored 22 and is leading the goal-scoring pack. But the next day things come screeching to a halt. They are playing Chelsea and it's the 73rd minute. The fans are focused on whoever is taking the corner, but in the centre of the box Blues number 2 Branislav Ivanović is on the ground. It is only when the televised replay shows the pitch from another angle that it becomes clear what has happened. Luis and his opponent were chasing the ball. They push and tug at one another, and when the ball has already rolled far away, Suárez gets hold of the Serbian player's arm and bites it. The 'cannibal' strikes again, this time at Anfield.

Once again, the whole country turns on him. And the punishment is a ten-match ban. On 26 April, Luis explains that he has decided not to appeal the decision: 'I accept that the act was not acceptable. I am not appealing because I do not want to give the wrong impression to people.' When the dust settles, he elaborates in an interview with Uruguay TV: 'I was angry about having gifted a penalty to Chelsea. I saw red and was out of it. I do not know how to explain it but I realise I made a mistake. It is solely my fault. Ivanović did not do anything to me.'

The next few months are far from easy, and in addition he hasn't been hiding his desire to move to an even bigger team. He wants to play in the Champions League and Liverpool have been falling short in that regard. Eventually things settle down, and on 29 September 2013, 161 days after the bite against Chelsea, Luis is back to scoring for the Reds, netting two against Sunderland. He celebrates by lifting his shirt to reveal a T-shirt with a picture of Benjamin, his second child, born four days earlier.

As the weeks pass, Liverpool are becoming unstoppable. On 8 February 2014 at Anfield they revel in one of the best victories of the season when they put four past Arsenal in just nineteen minutes. They make the Gunners look slow and cumbersome and Wenger's men go home after a 5-1 defeat – a crushing blow to their dreams of glory. Liverpool, on the other hand, can dare to dream about reclaiming the Premier League. It's the start of an eleven-match-winning streak.

On 27 April Luis receives the PFA Player of the Year 2013-14 award, confirming this as his comeback year. He is the first non-European to win the trophy, and it's all down to his 30 league goals. Sadly, things end in tears less than two weeks later when the Reds draw with Crystal Palace, putting an end to any hopes of taking the title.

It's time for Luis to bid England farewell. He leaves without any titles, but with a spectacular season under his belt. In his mind's eye he is already several hundred miles away.

Chapter 5

Club managers' views

'In Uruguay, there are 3 million coaches, critics and sports commentators. Each has their own opinion, their own formation, their tactics, their favourite forward, but Luis Suárez has made everyone agree for once.'

Rubén Sosa is one of the people who knows Barça's newest signing the best. The ex-forward for Danubio, Nacional, Real Zaragoza, Lazio, Inter, Borussia Dortmund, Logroñés and Shanghai Shenhua recalls how he met Lucho: 'It was when I came back from Spain, from Logroñés. I was playing for Nacional, he was in the youth teams, then I trained him for a bit when he was promoted to the first team. I was assistant coach for the forwards. I remember I told him that he wanted to score too quickly, he was always pushing ahead, looking for the goal. He wanted to win, and that was why he missed goals. In the first few matches he missed about twelve chances. I told him to relax and that when he scored the first goal, the rest would follow. He just had to be patient.'

But that's not all Sosa has to teach him. With him Luis learns to play with his back to the goal before spinning round and shooting, or heading a cross in on an angle. 'All kids in South America, including here in Uruguay, are born with a ball under their arm, as a football is the first thing that a parent used to buy their son,' he continues. 'Daughters would get a Barbie. Times have changed but there is no greater present than a football. A PlayStation will not even get a look in. It is this first present that ignites the passion for the beautiful game. But if you want to make it your living, you need to work hard.'

And that's exactly what Luis does, despite some difficult early years. 'He was so stressed that he never managed to convert it and people would whistle at him. They called him *loco* – crazy – but in the good sense of the word,' says Sosa. 'But all the shouting, whistling and insults never bothered him. He just wanted to be a good player, he wanted to play at Nacional, because it was the club of his dreams, and he got there, with a huge amount of effort and sacrifice.'

Nacional coach Martín Lasarte, who was the one who put him in the first team, has similar memories: 'I never understood why they had it in for him. It all started with the match against River. Luis created ten or twelve chances but messed up the final pass, the shot. He failed to put the ball in the back of the net. The insults started but Luis managed to quell the critics. His goals and moves saw to that. By the end of the season he was an idol for the fans.'

Lasarte himself is one of the living legends of Uruguayan football, winning the Copa Libertadores, Intercontinental, Interamericana and Recopa Sudamericana. But he always saw something special in Suárez. 'He was shy but with a great personality. He seemed much more mature than his age. I believe he was forced to grow up before his time, considering what was going on in his personal life. He was from central Uruguay, he had to fight for his family, bring home the dough, make his way in a big city like Montevideo and make it in football. One thing for sure, he believed in himself, he was sure of his abilities.'

Across the pond, in the Netherlands, it's the same story. 'He had a strong personality, he was an open book and very frank. What you see is what you get,' says Henk ten Cate, El Pistolero's first manager at Ajax. 'Luis didn't hold anything back. He was and is a winner, you could see it in his face. He was a kid from the streets who had learnt how to fight to survive and he showed it on the pitch, giving his heart and soul for every ball. Obviously he had to adapt to the club, to its discipline and to the pressure that was loaded on his shoulders. If you win at Groningen, great, if you lose, it's not the end of world. At Ajax, you have to win every match, every competition and the league. If you don't, it's a failure.'

Nonetheless, the Dutch coach admits that the club had serious doubts about him in the early days: 'We paid dearly for Luis, 7.5 million euros, which is a high price for the Dutch market, especially for a young player who has yet to prove his worth. As had happened with lots of other kids of his age at the club, there was a risk that he would not flourish, that he would not continue what he had started at Groningen.' But it is the opposite with Luis, particularly after forward Klaas-Jan Huntelaar leaves for Real Madrid. 'Huntelaar and Suárez were two roosters in the chicken coop fighting for the number 1 spot,' explains Henk ten Cate.

The pair overlapped for barely four months, but the coach still has not forgotten what he said to him before he left. 'I told him to be himself, to believe in his dreams and to not change his attitude on the pitch. For someone like Luis, all a coach can do is try to teach him tactics. You cannot tell him how to play the ball, he learnt that on the streets of Salto and Montevideo.'

On one thing all of Luis's former coaches agree: El Salteño immerses himself in football with a passion. 'It is this way of interpreting the game that has made him a great player,' says Uruguayan Ricardo Perdomo, who has played for teams such as Nacional and River Plate, and worked alongside Luis between 2002 and 2005. He knows everything there is to know about him

– good and bad. But he doesn't judge him: 'He has made mistakes due to his temperament. But he knows when he has done wrong. When all's said and done, who doesn't make mistakes in life?'

* * *

Dorival Silvestre Júnior could ask the very same question. The former Santos coach experienced the worst of Neymar – the 'monster', as he began to be called after his tantrum against Goianiense – who, in the process of becoming the fans' idol, seemed dangerously tempted by all the trappings of the football superstar lifestyle: 'Parties, girls, every kind of temptation,' says the coach.

He found fame overnight, which was very difficult for such a young kid to deal with. 'When I arrived at Santos in December 2009 Neymar was not that well known. He had just started in the first team about six months earlier,' Dorival Júnior explains. 'In January I met him by chance in a shopping centre while he was shopping with his girlfriend, just like lots of kids his age. He was just wandering around without anyone bothering him or asking for his autograph or a photo. By the April, he finished training on pitch 1 and on pitch 2 there was a helicopter waiting to take him to Rio or São Paulo for a publicity event or TV show. In three months, his life had changed completely.'

But what does a coach do when faced with such

a rich, famous and powerful young star? 'I got his attention. I spoke to him and said that he needed to focus on football, training and his work ethic because the demands he would face on the pitch would get harder and harder with each game. I told him that at the end of the day, that was his job.' The Goianiense incident might have ended with the coach leaving the dugout, but even now, with the benefit of hindsight, not only does he not regret his decision, he believes it was an important lesson for the kid as much as for him. 'Neymar matured thanks to the reaction of his family and his friends. He understood the seriousness of what he had done and what was happening to him. He grew up a lot, he grew as a player and as a person. He went back to his roots, to normality. It was a key moment in his career. A jump forward.'

After Dorival's departure, Muricy Ramalho arrives in the Peixe dugout. He only has one criticism of Ney: his taste in music. As for the rest, it's all positive: 'He is respectful and polite. He turns up to training and shakes your hand and says hello to everyone at all levels in the club. He is very friendly with people. His hair, his clothes and his practical jokes made people think he was a bit of a rebel, but they were wrong. He is a kid with his feet firmly on the ground, who always listens to his father, his trainers and his physio. He is completely focused on his job. I'll give you an example: my flat was at the training centre in Santos.

Sometimes I would wake up at two or three in the morning and his car was in the car park. He had just finished a TV advert in São Paulo or Rio, and instead of going home to his mother and father he would come straight to the club so that he could start his day's work. He would have breakfast and then go straight to training. No one asked him to, he just did it because he's a professional.'

Ramalho has no doubts about Ney's future: 'He will reach Messi's level. It will happen gradually and naturally, like a handing over, as happened with Ronaldinho and Messi. Neymar is preparing himself for this role. His objectives are clear and he will achieve them. He is not the sort of player who thinks that if things go well then that's fine but if they go badly then that's fine too. He wants to be the best player in the world. He does not talk about it but he thinks about it. I know this is the case. He has the personality to do it.'

* * *

There is a crucial attribute that Neymar, Leo and Luis have in common: they all give the impression that they are really enjoying themselves. 'The pleasure of playing,' as Frank Rijkaard puts it. 'It doesn't matter if he is playing in front of ten spectators or 100,000. Leo is the same as always, he always feels secure and has the same desire to win,' says the former Barça coach. 'He is the boy who says: "Give me the ball, I want to

play, I want to be creative, I want to show my talents."
And when he gets it, it's a difficult task to stop him
without fouling him. He is extremely fast, he has great
ball control, an exquisite touch and he can dribble in
a way rarely seen throughout the footballing world.
And let's not forget, he's explosive, and although he's
not very tall, he is very strong. You can see it when he
clashes with the opposition – it's not easy to knock
him down.'

The Dutchman doesn't hide the affection he still
feels for Lionel, who made his debut with the first
team during his tenure: 'When he debuted he was a
very well balanced person, calm, respectful and very
shy. Over time, he has changed a lot, but without losing these attributes. Now he is more sure of himself,
he is conscious of being an important player in the
team. Everyone values him and he is perfectly aware
of it. His attitude has not changed, but he is not the
silent boy he was all those years ago. He is funnier, he
likes to joke around when he is with his teammates or
surrounded by people he knows … I have to say that
from day one the team has behaved very well towards
him, the group has accepted him. Sylvinho, Deco,
Ronaldinho, they've helped and advised him. Great
players always recognise a special player.'

Álex García also has positive memories of the
Argentine, whom he trained in the Barça youth A
team: 'Messi was very receptive, always attentive to

everything, quiet, shy, reserved, with great class,' he says. 'He was a different type of player, when he got the ball he was unstoppable, he had a devastating side-step. He would get annoyed on the pitch if you didn't pass it to him, or if he didn't do as well as he wanted, but he never argued over a referee's decision or over a foul.'

And he never uttered a word of complaint about living far from his home, his mother and his siblings: 'I knew that he was far from home, from his family, that he lived here with his father. I could imagine his nostalgia. Sometimes I asked him about it, but he acted like nothing bothered him. He held everything inside. At fifteen years of age, Leo already knew what he wanted, he was conscious of the fact that he had an opportunity at Barça, he knew what it meant to make a sacrifice – both his sacrifice and his family's, and he didn't want to waste the opportunity he had been given.'

It seems as though he was the perfect kid. But like everyone, he must have had a weakness. Just one, admits García – he didn't like playing out of position. 'He never said anything, but you could see it on his face.' In fact, the coach tried to move him around to broaden his skill set, from centre forward, to the wing ... but 'after a few minutes he would drift back towards the centre, into the hole. There was nothing you could do about it.'

Adrián Coria also struggles to remember ever seeing a negative side to the Flea. 'He was respectful. He paid attention. He never said "I'm playing", he never said "I'm the best". His teammates adored him,' says the man who coached Leo at Newell's Old Boys in the youth leagues. 'The only thing was ... he didn't like exercises. He loved the ball. That's why I once had to send him off during training. I'm not an ogre or a sergeant major, but I've always liked people to take things seriously. We were doing a lap, and he kept playing around with the ball. I called to him once, twice, but it was like he took no notice ... Finally I said to him: "Give me the ball, get changed and go home." Ten minutes later I saw him with his bag on his shoulder, glued to the wire fence, watching the pitch. I felt bad and it saddened me to see him like that. "You left without saying goodbye," I yelled over to him. He came over to say goodbye and I sent him back to the changing room so that he could rejoin the practice. He was a shy kid with a tough character, but that was the only time I had to say something to him.'

Summing him up, Coria adds: 'He was a Gardel.' A legend, like the celebrated tango singer Carlos Gardel, another Argentine national hero.

Chapter 6

National team

Neymar marks his national team debut with a goal –
Messi and Suárez with a sending off.

* * *

Luis's adventure with the Celeste (Sky Blues) begins
on 7 February 2007. Uruguay are playing a friendly
against Colombia at the General Santander stadium
in Cúcuta. It's an opportunity for manager Óscar
Wáshington Tabárez to experiment and try out the
up and coming players – including Lucho, who is just
twenty years old.

He goes on wearing the number 10. This is his
moment. In the thirteenth minute, he beats the line
of defence and charges towards the Colombian goal,
chasing after a long pass behind the defenders which
catches them by surprise. He cuts into the area and
is about to shoot, but goalie Miguel Calero, instead
of blocking the ball, goes for his feet. Penalty. Calero
is sent off and Sebastián Abreu converts the kick in
the seventeenth minute. Another penalty by Abreu in

the 60th minute takes the score to 2-0. Uruguay win
3-1, but Lucho is not there for the final whistle after
receiving a second yellow card in the 85th minute.
He had been giving Jorge Hernán Hoyos too much
lip for an earlier decision, and the ref sends him for
an early shower.

After his debut with the first team, it's time for the
FIFA Under-20 World Cup in Canada. But unfortunately for Luis and his teammates they are knocked
out in the first round. His next outing in the national
shirt is on 12 September at Ellis Park in Johannesburg,
in a friendly against South Africa. It's an uneventful
fixture, but it's an important one for Suárez because
from that moment on he is always on Tabárez's teamsheet. A month later, on 13 October, he scores his first
international goal, at Uruguay's Centenario stadium,
against Bolivia. It's the first CONMEBOL (South
American Football Confederation) qualifier for the
2010 South Africa World Cup. Luis sends the ball flying towards the goal in the fourth minute, and the
goalkeeper can't hold onto it. Martín Lasarte is in the
crowd and, despite not being one for shouting, Luis's
former coach at Nacional lets out a cry of joy when the
ball hits the back of the net.

Suárez plays nineteen out of twenty World Cup
qualifiers, scoring against Chile, Venezuela, Colombia
and Ecuador. The goals against Colombia and
Ecuador are particular cause for celebration. But in

the final few fixtures his goal-scoring efforts dry up. He will later admit that it was a difficult time. But Uruguay still manage to squeeze through. And on 18 November 2009, Luis is on the pitch celebrating with a 70,000-strong crowd at the Centenario after a hard-fought 1-1 draw puts them through. After coming fifth in the South American qualifiers, the Celeste have had to wait it out through the playoffs, but it has been worth all the hard work.

The first African World Cup turns Luis into the Celeste's newest star – with apologies to Diego Forlán.

His international career is in the ascendant, and really begins to take off a year later during the 2011 Copa América – football's oldest continental tournament. It was first played in Buenos Aires in 1916 to celebrate the centenary of Argentina's declaration of independence. Uruguay's Celeste won and Argentina's Albiceleste (White and Sky Blues) came second – a blight on the host nation's record.

The humiliation is to be repeated in 2011 when Uruguay knock them out. The Celeste go on to win it, taking their tally to fifteen, one more than the Argentines. It is an unforgettable moment for the citizens of the Eastern Republic. The two rivals meet in the quarter-final – an agonising match that pits Messi against Suárez. It goes to penalties, and Uruguay have been playing with ten men since the 38th minute following Diego Pérez's sending off. Luis will later say that it was the toughest game of his career. But the Celeste win, the worst is over.

The semi-final against Peru is Lucho's international coming of age party, thanks to his two goals. And on 24 July, in the final against Paraguay at River Plate's Monumental stadium, he does it again. He gets a long ball from Ruso Pérez in the eleventh minute, darts into the box, dodges and feints round the defender and pings the ball in off the post: 1-0. El Pistolero shoots his finger 'guns' towards the crowd before diving on the pitch and being smothered by his teammates. The crowd goes wild, chanting 'Suárez, Suárez'.

Forlán then decides to join the goal-scoring party after a dry spell with the Celeste of more than a year. Arévalo Ríos steals the ball from Ortizoga and offers it up to the number 10. Diego shoots to make it 2-0. He later finishes out the goal-scoring with a great effort in the 89th minute: Celeste counter-attack, Suárez assist, and goal number three. Uruguay are the champions of America. And Luis is the FIFA player of the competition.

On 30 June 2013, Lucho and his teammates repeat their South Africa success in the FIFA Confederations Cup in Brazil, coming fourth behind the host nation, Spain and Italy.

* * *

And it is in that very tournament – the second most

important after the World Cup – that Neymar goes head to head with El Salteño and becomes the Brazilian Canaries' new leader.

In the first Confederations Cup match, against Japan on 15 June at the Mané Garrincha stadium, Neymar scores his first goal after just three minutes. Marcelo crosses from the left, Fred controls it on his chest and, with the ball still in the air, Neymar connects with his right foot, sending the ball flying into the top corner of the net at 98 kilometres an hour. Things could not be off to a better start.

On 19 June, before the second match, the Barça player shows his support for public protests that have been going on for weeks across Brazil, writing on his Facebook page: 'Let's wave our flags in favour of the protests that are happening across Brazil. I'm BRAZILIAN and I love my country! I have family and friends who live in Brazil. For that reason, I also want a more just, safe, healthy and HONEST Brazil! The only way I can represent and defend Brazil is by playing football. But, starting from this match against Mexico, I will go out onto the pitch inspired by this incredible public protest.'

And he is decisive once again – in fact it is more or less a one-man show. After nine minutes, a cross from Dani Alves, deflected by Rodriguez, meets Neymar's punishing volley. Then in the 90th minute, he catches the Mexican defence off guard and delivers the ball on a plate to Jô, who makes it two. Mexico are out, and Neymar is man of the match for the second time.

Brazil's final Group A match is against Italy in Salvador da Bahia on 22 June. The match ends 4-2, with Neymar Júnior scoring the second, although the Canaries aren't particularly convincing. Regardless, they are through to the semis, and now they have to face Suárez and Uruguay. But it's a disappointing duel. The play drags and there is not much good football. The Celeste dominate the second half, but luck falls on the side of the Canaries, who manage to seal a 2-1 win four minutes before the end of extra time. Ney doesn't score, although he sets up both his team's goals.

One week later, it's the hotly anticipated final: Brazil vs Spain. And Neymar is on fire. He has a hand in the first goal, scored by Fred just a minute and 33 seconds into the game. And he scores the second following an explosive counter-attack just before the half-time whistle. Another one from Fred after the break makes it a definitive 3-0.

Juninho leaves the Maracanã stadium with the champions' medal, the Golden Ball for best player and the Bronze Boot for the third-highest goal-scorer of the tournament. An incredible achievement for a kid who only debuted with the national team three years earlier. His first outing was against the USA in New Meadowlands, New Jersey, on 10 August 2010.

It was quite the baptism of fire, as he scored the first of Brazil's two goals with a header in the 28th minute.

From that moment on, he would get a great deal of enjoyment from playing for the Canaries. Like winning the 2011 Sudamericano Under-20 tournament, or taking silver in the Olympic Games the following year.

He would also experience some unforgettable moments, like the Brazil-Argentina friendly in Doha on 17 November 2010. Neymar, Ronaldinho and Messi on one pitch. Ney cannot contain his excitement – although, of course, most of the attention is on the two great friends and former Barça teammates, the Gaucho and the Flea.

* * *

At least that 2010 friendly in Doha is a chance for Messi to get even, beating his eternal rivals the Canaries on the fifth attempt. The previous contests had seen Argentina lose three and draw one. Even at the Beijing Olympics in 2008, when Argentina beat Brazil on the way to the gold medal, Messi had not managed to score in the match. This time he scores in the 47th minute after an unbelievable slalom through the defence.

Messi is already the crucial cog in the Albiceleste line-up by this point. It has been five years since he made his international debut, on 17 August 2005, in a friendly against Hungary at the Ferenc Puskás stadium in Budapest. On that occasion he came on for Maxi López in the 65th minute. And he is on the pitch for little more than 40 seconds. On his second touch, he dribbles the ball past Vanczák. The Hungarian grabs him by his brand-new number 18 shirt. Messi lifts his arm and pushes him back. Bam! He catches the defender full in the face. German referee Markus Merk is in no doubt. He elbowed him. And he pulls out the red card in front of the disbelieving Argentines. Sent off in his first match. Not the scenario that Leo had imagined. He is to spend the rest of the match crying. His coach and teammates think the referee's decision is excessive, but their words of consolation are in vain.

An unfortunate debut, without a doubt. Particularly considering he arrived in the first team with incredible credentials, after winning the Under-20 World Cup in the Netherlands. But it is going to be tough settling in. He is extremely shy and he doesn't communicate much with his teammates or coaches. Let's not forget that he is very young – he has only just turned eighteen. It's going to be a long process, but by the time of the 2008 Beijing Olympic Games he feels comfortable, with the Under-23 team at least. He seems to get on best with Kun Agüero, with whom he shares a room and a penchant for PlayStation. He has had a difficult time persuading Barça to let him take part, and FIFA have had to intervene, but finally he gets to go to China.

In the first match against the Ivory Coast he helps his team to a 2-1 victory. Next the Albiceleste dispense with Australia, then Serbia – although Leo is rested for that one – and then the Netherlands.

In the semi-final it's the great duel, the *Clásico par excellence*: Argentina-Brazil. Or rather, Messi versus Ronaldinho. The present versus the past, the current star against the champion who is looking to rise from the ashes. This time it is Argentina's turn to get the win, but in a way that nobody could have imagined. They quash, humiliate and make fun of Brazil. Agüero scores two goals and has a hand in the third after he is fouled and Riquelme converts the penalty. He celebrates by miming putting a dummy in his mouth, as his fiancée Giannina is expecting. It all just serves to highlight the weakness of Dunga's Canaries and Ronaldinho's decline.

But even more cruel is the photo that appears in the media across the world the following day: Ronnie in his yellow number 10 shirt and captain's armband, finding solace, head bowed, in the arms of his 'little brother' Messi. Lionel is standing on tiptoes in order to console his idol. There is a lot of affection in that picture, but there is also a lot of melancholy. Without making a big impression, Leo has won that highly anticipated duel. He is happy. Ronnie only wants to hide, to disappear from the face of the earth.

On to the final. At noon on Saturday 23 August

(1.00am in Argentina) at the National Stadium, nicknamed the Bird's Nest, the final of the Olympic Games football tournament begins. Argentina are up against Nigeria, just like in Atlanta '96 and in the 2005 Under-20 World Cup in the Netherlands. In the American Olympics, Nwankwo Kanu's Nigeria took home the gold after a 3-2 final, considered by FIFA to be one of the ten most memorable matches in a century of Olympic football. But Argentina get their revenge in 2005. And the protagonist on that occasion, the one who defeats the Green Eagles, is Lionel, with two penalties.

But the 2008 final in Beijing is dull and boring, and twice the referee calls for a basketball-style time-out due to the oppressive heat. Finally, in the 57th minute, there is a scuffle between an Argentine and a Nigerian, the ball rebounds towards the centre of the pitch, Messi recovers it, turns, and passes it perfectly, out deep, to Ángel Di María. The ex-Rosario Central midfielder, currently at Manchester United, the sensation of the Games, gallops away freely on the left. And on the edge of the area, in front of Vanzekin who desperately comes off his line, he is inspired to lift the ball softly with his left foot and send it lightly through the heavy Beijing air. The Nigerian goalkeeper can do nothing but get up and, motionless in the penalty area, watch from afar as the ball bounces into the net – a work of art that deserves the gold.

Chapter 7

High points

Although football stars are accustomed to victory, there will always be special days, unique memories and unforgettable experiences that stand out above the rest. These are life's magic moments.

Messi: four FIFA Ballon d'Or awards

Yes – this time, it's his turn. This time, the saying 'third time lucky' is accurate. After coming third in 2007 and second in 2008, Lionel Andrés Messi wins France Football magazine's 2009 Ballon d'Or. And he wins it by a mile, garnering 473 out of a possible 480 points, more than double the score of runner-up Cristiano Ronaldo, who is awarded 233 points. Xavi Hernández comes third with 173 points. Ninety of the award's 96 voters vote for Leo as their number one player, and with 98.54 per cent of the maximum number of points possible, nobody in the 54-year history of this prestigious prize has won it as convincingly or unanimously as Messi. It is a real triumph.

All sides are united in agreement on Messi's

records, performances, talent, class and professional career. The journalists of France Football's international voting panel have all bowed to the Flea. Tributes have poured in from around the world: from Japan to Iceland, from Ghana to New Zealand, from Kazakhstan to England.

Lionel is the first footballer who has trained through Barça's La Masia youth academy to lift the Ballon d'Or. 'This prize is an honour. It is wonderful and very special, but I wasn't obsessed with winning it. I knew that if it was meant to happen it would, but either way I would keep on working in the same way as always,' he says in the Nou Camp press room. A few days later in Paris he makes a confession that, though unexpected, is not surprising: 'I would love to win it again. It would be magnificent to win one more.'

And he doesn't have to wait long. Twelve months later in Zurich, the cameras zoom in on Leo Messi, Andrés Iniesta and Xavi Hernández, the three finalists of the 2010 Ballon d'Or, all from Barcelona. It's an unprecedented trifecta in Blaugrana history, testament to the club's style and teaching traditions. An emotional Pep Guardiola opens the envelope to reveal the winner … and the Flea goes up on stage once again to receive his prize. But the decision is not without controversy this year. Not only have Iniesta and Xavi enjoyed an impressive title haul with Barça this year, they also won the South Africa World

Cup with Spain. But the judges have spoken: Leo is the best.

One year later, he does it again. Brazil's Ronaldo is charged with opening the envelope to reveal the winner of the 2011 Ballon d'Or. And this time there are neither surprises nor controversies. The Flea takes his third trophy, equalling the tallies of Michel Platini (1983, 1984, 1985), Johan Cruyff (1971, 1972, 1974) and Marco van Basten (1988, 1989, 1992). He has entered the hall of fame.

Naturally, someone so accustomed to smashing record after record is not going to stop there. On 7 January 2013, Leo becomes the only player to win four Ballon d'Or trophies – and four consecutive trophies to boot. It was a little more unexpected this time, particularly for the man himself. 'It hasn't been my best year,' he acknowledges at the press conference. When Italy's Fabio Cannavaro announces his name, the Barça number 10 receives a huge ovation. He has received 41.6 per cent of the votes, beating Cristiano Ronaldo's 23.68 per cent and Iniesta's 10.91 per cent. The Flea's 91 goals have counted for more than Cristiano's Liga or Supercup victories with Real, or Iniesta's UEFA Euro 2012 trophy with Spain. He goes up on stage dressed in a rather loud black and white polka dot Dolce & Gabbana jacket and bow tie, a world away from the sober suit he wore when he won it the first time around. The Flea has gone through a metamorphosis in every sense: he is gaining in confidence – and not just with the ball.

In the last ten years at Barcelona, Messi has gone from promising youngster to the most celebrated footballer in recent history. He is the top goal-scorer in the club's history, and he is also the top scorer in Barça-Real Madrid *Clásicos*, with a tally of 21. To date he has six Liga victories, three Champions League trophies, two Copa del Rey wins, six Spanish Supercups, two UEFA Super Cups and two Club World Cups – a dizzying array of individual and collective achievements.

Neymar: 2011 FIFA Puskás Award for goal of the year

On 9 January 2012, Neymar arrives at Zurich's Congress Palace, where the annual FIFA gala is held. He sits in one of the front rows, wearing a black jacket, white shirt and grey tie, sporting red highlights in his hair. He is one of the star attractions: nominated for the Puskás Award and shortlisted for the Ballon d'Or.

Co-host Ruud Gullit reads out the awards on the stage. The other two Puskás finalists are Messi and Wayne Rooney: the Argentine for his Champions League goal against Arsenal on 8 March, a fantastic flick and volley to beat the Gunners' keeper, and the Manchester United centre-forward for his overhead kick in the derby against Man City on 12 February.

And Ney? The youngster is being recognised along-side the big names thanks to his incredible Brasileirão league goal against Flamengo on 27 July. The Peixe end up losing 4-5, but it is Neymar's greatest match with his childhood club. He engineers two goals, the first of which is a work of art. He receives the ball near the touchline, just inside the Flamengo half. Leo Moura and Williams have been marking him closely, and are beginning to close in. He needs to get out into open space. It looks impossible but somehow he manages it, slipping between the two and running forward. He sees Borges and plays a one-two. Renato is closing in but Neymar skims round him and then moves on to take on Ronaldo Angelim. A bit of drib-bling and then the masterpiece: a flick to one side and Ney dodges around the other side of him. With a few metres to go, he can see the defenders diving in and the goalkeeper coming off his line, and lobs it into the back of the net.

The videos of all three goals are shown, and then journalist and co-host Kate Murray introduces Hugo Sánchez, the greatest Mexican player of all time, who will present the award. The former Real Madrid player comments: 'Scoring a beautiful goal makes you very happy but receiving this award is the best. I speak from experience.' The TV cameras zoom in on Messi, Neymar and Rooney. 'The FIFA Puskás Award for 2011 goes to … Neymar.'

The kid from Santos removes his earphones (worn for translation purposes) and shakes Rooney's hand. He gets up and passes Gerard Piqué and Iniesta. He buttons his jacket and goes up on stage, greeting Sánchez, Gullit and Murray, before addressing the audience. 'I am very happy to have been given this award. I was up against two of the greatest stars in football, of whom I am a big fan. I want to thank God and all those who are here. Have a great night,' says an emotional Neymar. He accepts his award and heads off to party.

Just like Messi, the kid from Mogi das Cruzes is quickly becoming accustomed to garnering recognition and awards. At just 22 he already has quite a few to his name. After winning the Puskás in 2011, he is nominated again the following year and comes third. In 2011 and 2012 he is named Brazilian player of the year, and he has won three Golden Boot awards, in 2010, 2011 and 2012, for scoring the most goals across all Brazilian competitions. In 2011 FIFA names him the most valuable young player in the world, and in 2013 he wins the Confederations Cup Golden Ball. He is named best player in the 2011 Copa Libertadores and the 2012 Recopa Sudamericana. He is part of the Americas fantasy eleven, and Uruguayan newspaper *El País* votes him the best American footballer in 2012 and 2013. And as if that's not enough, he is Brazil's best-ever Olympic goal-scorer.

Messi representing Barcelona in October 2004, aged seventeen. Despite his Argentinian birth and upbringing, Barça has been his only senior club, and in more than a decade there he has set records that may never be broken.

Francesc Valcarcel/Press Association Images

Neymar Jr, on the other hand, played his early football in Brazil with Santos, winning six trophies between 2010 and 2012. Here, he and his teammates celebrate a goal in the 2011 Copa Libertadores final.

AP Photo/Andre Penner

Suárez's career has been considerably more nomadic than those of his fellow Barça forwards, starting in Uruguay with Nacional (left) and taking in stints with Groningen, Ajax and Liverpool (right), before the Blaugrana came calling.

Messi leads Argentina out for the 2014 World Cup final. FIFA would name him as their player of the tournament, but it was Germany who would prevail to win their fourth World Cup.

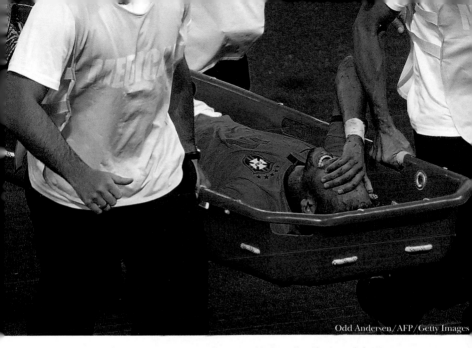

Brazil's great hope and inspiration Neymar had earlier departed the tournament in agony after a challenge by Colombia's Juan Zúñiga left him with a broken vertebra (above). Even more bizarrely, Suárez was sent home in disgrace after biting Italy's Giorgio Chiellini (below).

After a lengthy ban, Suárez finally makes his competitive debut for the Blaugrana – the small matter of Real Madrid at the Bernabeu.

Neymar, Messi and Suárez celebrate with their teammate Andrés Iniesta as the goals start to flow for Barça's new-look attack.

Luis Suárez: European Golden Shoe 2013-14

For the purposes of this particular comparison, Luis Suárez will have to make do with third place, at least for now. But make no mistake, like his Blaugrana teammates, he is just as accustomed to receiving international recognition for his footballing feats. In 2010 he is named Dutch footballer of the year, and becomes the highest goal-scorer in the Eredivisie and in Europe, netting 49 goals in 48 matches across all competitions. For three consecutive years, from 2008 to 2010, he racks up the most assists in the Dutch top division. In 2009 and 2010 he is named Ajax's best player and top goal-scorer, which he will repeat the following two seasons at Liverpool. He is also twice selected in the Premier League fantasy eleven. When Uruguay win the Copa América in 2011, Luis is named man of the match in the final, as well as player of the tournament. Two years later, during the Confederations Cup, he becomes Uruguay's all-time top goal-scorer, overtaking Diego Forlán and Héctor Scarone. His current tally stands at 43 goals. In 2014 he is named both the Barclays Premier League Player of the Season and the Golden Boot.

And then there is the 2013-14 European Golden Shoe, which is awarded by European Sports Media to the top goal-scorer across all the European leagues. It's a particularly special prize because it comes during one of the most difficult times in his career, following the Chiellini biting incident. He shares the award with Cristiano Ronaldo, although the Real star will receive his trophy several weeks later at a different presentation. They have both scored 31 league goals, beating Messi, who won it the previous two years.

Lucho's ceremony is on 15 October 2014 at the old Estrella Damm factory in Barcelona. He arrives with wife Sofia at 6.30pm. Barça president Josep Maria Bartomeu, sporting director Andoni Zubizarreta and some of Luis's Uruguayan teammates are also there. Xavi Hernández, Andrés Iniesta and Sergio Busquets are seated in the front row. Further back sits a smiling Pere Guardiola, who is Lucho's agent – and brother of former Barça coach Pep.

There is also an emotional reunion in store, as Luis has requested that Kenny Dalglish be the person to present him with the trophy. The Liverpool legend was responsible for bringing El Pistolero to the club during his tenure as manager, and Luis has won the Golden Shoe because of his performance with the Reds. 'He has been fantastic, I don't think there will be anybody who will be able to stop him,' Dalglish says, before presenting him with the trophy that only one Uruguayan has won before him – ex-Atlético Madrid forward Diego Forlán.

But that is not the only special moment. Sofia also gets to speak, and in a voice trembling with emotion she explains what the award means to their family:

'The children and I are so incredibly proud of him. We know what he has been through and this prize comes at the end of a difficult year.'

It is only a 30 minute presentation, but it represents the light at the end of the tunnel for Luis Suárez. He says he feels 'proud'.

As a final thought, he says that if he had to choose his favourite goal, he knows which it would be: his third in the match against Norwich City in April 2012 – an incredible shot from the halfway line. Liverpool won that match 3-0 thanks to his hat-trick. It doesn't matter that he hasn't chosen one of the 31 goals in the 2013-14 season that won him the Golden Shoe. For Luis that goal represents the best of his past with Liverpool, and with that, it's time to move on.

Chapter 8

Low points

Even superstars have their off days, and Suárez, Ney and Messi are no exception. They too know what it's like to fall from grace, they have experienced criticism and disaffection. Here we take a look at their darkest hours, the controversies that have overshadowed the sport and thrust them into the glare of the media spotlight.

Suárez: World Cup bite

Lucho's infamous biting of Italy's Giorgio Chiellini has caused the biggest footballing furore in recent memory. It seems as though the entire planet knows what happened during the match in Natal on 24 June 2014. That's the thing about the World Cup – everyone is watching, not just the die-hard fans.

In the days following the incident, Suárez is all anyone can talk about. The tournament itself takes a back seat. It's a trending topic. Plenty of people defend him, and there are even those who, like Uruguayan president Pepe Mújica, claim that there is no evidence among the TV footage of any aggression, only a 'vilifying campaign' against the player. Others try to rationalise the situation, suggesting that the 'cannibalistic' impulses must be due to some kind of childhood trauma. The harshest headlines are those in the British press: 'Three bites and you're out', 'Jaws III', 'Make biter Suárez a pariah' and 'Ban this monster' are just a few of the witty and not-so-witty headlines.

Just after 11.00am on 26 June 2014, FIFA makes a statement about the incident. Luis receives a nine-match ban at international level and a general four-month ban, plus a fine of 100,000 Swiss francs. The disciplinary committee says he has breached article 48 (aggressive and violent conduct) and article 57 (act of unsporting behaviour towards another player) of the FIFA disciplinary code. The sanction is applicable with immediate effect, meaning Suárez will miss the final sixteen match against Colombia, and any subsequent World Cup matches. If Uruguay go out of the World Cup, he will miss the team's next eight official matches instead. The four-month ban means he cannot take part in any footballing activity, whether administrative or sporting, as required by article 22 of the disciplinary code. As per article 21, during the ban he will not be able to access the stadiums where Uruguay play, and will have to leave the Uruguay training camp at Sete Lagoas. Committee chairman Claudio Sulser comments: 'Such behaviour cannot be tolerated on any football pitch, and in particular not at a FIFA World Cup when the eyes of millions of people are on the stars on the field.'

There has only been one similar ban based on televised evidence of an incident. In 1994 in the United States in the Italy-Spain quarter-final, Milan defender Mauro Tassotti elbowed Luis Enrique, breaking his nose, although the referee did not punish him at the time of the incident. The Blues went through to the semi-finals but FIFA saw the replay and decided to ban Tassotti for seven matches.

When the news breaks in Montevideo it's like a punch in the stomach. The country is paralysed in shock. No one was expecting Suárez to receive the most severe punishment in World Cup history. And there is just as much uproar outside Uruguay. Many people think it's excessive, including Diego Armando Maradona ('Who did Suárez kill? This is football, there is contact. Why don't they just handcuff him and send him straight to Guantanamo') and Brazil's Fred ('Suárez can't deny that he made a mistake but, as a player and a human being, I understand that in those moments your nerves are on edge and the fight for space in the box is intense. The ban seems a bit too harsh and unfair').

Even Chiellini himself seems to be on Lucho's side. 'Right now my only thoughts are for Luis and his family, because they are about to go through a very

difficult time,' the defender writes on his website. 'I
think the ban is excessive. I hope that at the very least
he'll be allowed to stay near his teammates during the
matches, because that sort of restriction would drive
any player mad.'

But former Brazil striker Ronaldo sees it differently:
'Football has to maintain that line of respect and act
as an example. Those who cross the line need to be
punished.'

Neymar: transfer controversy

Diehard Barça fan Jordi Cases is much more than a
season ticket holder on the Nou Camp terraces. The
forty-something pro-independence Catalan, who is
a pharmacist in a town around half an hour outside
Barcelona, has stirred up one of the most significant
institutional crises in the club's history. For better or
worse, his name will forever be linked with that of
Neymar Júnior.

He has single-handedly forced the dismissal of
Blaugrana president Sandro Rosell and pushed the
club to explain itself to shareholders and the courts,
in an attempt to reveal how much Barça paid for the
Brazilian player.

On 5 December 2013 Cases lodges a complaint
against Rosell with the Spanish national court for
alleged 'misappropriation of funds' during Neymar's
transfer. Cases is convinced the president has not

revealed the whole truth to shareholders about the signing and believes that the real amount paid is nearly double the official 57 million euro sum that was split between the four companies that had rights to the player: DIS, Teisa, Neymar Pai's company N&N Sports, and Santos.

Ever since Ney's presentation, there have been many who doubted that he could have been signed for such a 'low' amount. Even Real Madrid president Florentino Pérez claims he passed up the opportunity to buy the Brazilian player because it would allegedly have cost the Whites 150 million euros. But Barça continue to deny all the accusations and cite a confidentiality agreement to avoid revealing any further details.

After the Christmas break, events gather pace. Judge Pablo Ruz accepts the lawsuit against Rosell. It's official: the 'Neymar case' will proceed. According to the judge, Cases' claim contains 'sufficient basis' to investigate all the facts, since it 'could point to a contractual simulation carried out by those who signed the deal, which could indicate a lack of consistency between the original intention and the final agreements and financial obligations in the official signed contracts'. In other words, it is alleged that a parallel contract was signed in order to unofficially finance the transfer, even though that contract was officially for something else.

In addition, Ruz asks FIFA to provide any documentation relating to the signing, and requests that

Neymar provide his N&N contract relating to the relinquishing of future financial rights. He also sends an envoy to Brazil to obtain the player's work and transfer contracts, and requests that Barcelona provide the documents relating to the 7.9 million euros the club paid as an option on three young Santos players and the 9 million paid for two friendlies against Santos.

The following day, 21 January, Sandro Rosell resigns as president of FC Barcelona.

Following the resignation, vice-president Josep Maria Bartomeu takes the reins. Twenty-four hours later Barcelona admit for the first time that the total sum that changed hands for Neymar was some 86.2 million euros, excluding his salary. The signing was worth 57.1 million, while the rest corresponds to 'other items'. In particular, the services for which the footballer's father was paid – such as talent-spotting promising young Brazilian players – have been called into question, as it is alleged that such payments were a fraudulent way to purchase the player.

But why have Barça revealed the sum now? Because Neymar Pai has agreed to waive the confidentiality agreement. Nonetheless, the club stands by its earlier position that nothing untoward has occurred. Neither Santos nor DIS are convinced, however, and in light of the new figures now believe they should have received more money.

Meanwhile, the kid from Mogi das Cruzes prefers to stay well out of anything non-sport-related. But by 2 February he has had enough, and posts a picture and an explosive message online defending his father. 'I have kept quiet until now! But I can't bear to hear all these ridiculous things about my transfer any longer ... I'm sorry for disobeying you for the first time in my life, dad, but I have to speak out! I want to thank you for the way in which you have overseen my career, for the companies you created to support my work, and the way you have taken care of our family. If I previously played for my favourite team, and now I play for the team of my dreams, I owe it all to you. I know lots of people are talking a lot of rubbish about us, doubting us ... I have also realised how many fair-weather friends we have ... Dad, when Thiago Silva said he would die on the pitch for me, I thought the same about him ... But not only would I die for you, I would give my only son's life for you! So I'm begging you, come back to Spain, I miss you! I'll be back on the pitch in a few days and I need you here with me ... Time will show that you have done nothing wrong, that you have just been the best possible dad! I love you!'

At the end of the month, there is more bad news from the courts. The judge has charged Barcelona with suspected tax fraud relating to Neymar's signing. The club is said to owe the Inland Revenue more than

9 million euros. Barcelona insists on maintaining its innocence, but four days later decides to make a voluntary contribution of 13.5 million to the authorities. Overnight, Neymar's transfer has become worth more than 100 million euros. Barça tries to paint the payment as a gesture of goodwill 'given the existence of a possible divergent interpretation of the exact amount of tax responsibility arising from the signing' of the Brazilian. However, it is also likely that this payment will reduce any fine by some 60 per cent were the club to be found guilty.

On 2 October 2014, Neymar Pai testifies before a judge regarding his son's signing. On 21 October, Cases drops his case against Barça. The explanation offered is that there has been 'no evidence of illegal conduct in either corporate or financial dealings, or of embezzlement, nor is there any irregularity in the contracts and endorsements'.

But 'Neymargate' has been one of the biggest scandals in Blaugrana history, and it is not over yet. The case in the national court continues for now.

Messi: tax fraud allegations

The club's number 10 has also been pursued by the courts in recent years. On 27 September 2013, Leo arrives at the courthouse in Gava, a small municipality around 20 kilometres from Barcelona, and is greeted with cheers and applause from dozens of ardent fans.

One even calls out 'Messi for president!', while the occasional shout of criticism is well and truly drowned out. The Barça star responds with a thumbs-up. He is smiling and seems relaxed in a dark suit and white open-necked shirt.

It is just before 11.00am and Lionel is here to answer questions regarding three alleged counts of tax fraud between 2007 and 2009. The television cameras zoom in towards him to capture the moment. Both Messi and his father are accused of concocting an elaborate financial scheme to defraud the taxman. The authorities claim they transferred the footballer's image rights into shell companies registered in tax havens including Belize and Uruguay. They allegedly drew up 'licensing or service contracts between these companies and others registered in convenient jurisdictions', such as the UK and Switzerland.

The prosecutors say this enabled them to avoid tax payments on earnings from the player's various publicity deals with companies such as Adidas and Banco Sabadell, as well as FC Barcelona itself. It is alleged that they have made more than 10 million euros, of which 4.1 million is owed in unpaid tax.

The defence's strategy is to save Leo by allowing his father to assume responsibility. Jorge Messi is also due before the judge today. He has arrived just before his son, wearing rather a different expression: serious and distant, head bowed, eyes hidden behind sunglasses.

As expected, he insists that Lionel had absolutely nothing to do with the management of his image rights and tax issues. His aim is to resolve everything as quickly as possible. 'It is clear there is little desire to defraud and a great desire to clear up all the details with the Inland Revenue,' explains Cristóbal Martell, the Messis' lawyer.

On 16 December *El Mundo* leads with the shock headline: 'Messi's father investigated for laundering drug money'. The Civil Guard suspects that charitable 'Friends of Messi' matches could have been targeted by big-time drug traffickers as a way to launder money. The player's family strongly deny the accusations, and the investigators confirm that their inquiry does not centre on Jorge.

As far as those at Barcelona are concerned, it's yet another provocation intended to destabilise the club. The president thinks there are dark forces at work behind all these scandals surrounding his star player. 'The Barça leadership have had to put up with this for years. Of course it makes you stop and think, but I still want to do this. It's just a coincidence, nothing more,' declares Sandro Rosell – who will end up resigning a few days later over Neymargate.

So how are things looking now for the Argentine? At the beginning of October 2014 the judge rejects the player's appeal, which claimed that he had no knowledge of Jorge's actions. His defence ever since the scandal first broke has been: 'My dad takes care of the money.' The Flea and his father will face a trial, although they have made a voluntary contribution of 5 million euros to the Inland Revenue, which would reduce any eventual fine they could incur if found guilty.

In addition, the 'Friends of Messi' matches are under scrutiny once again. In June, *El País* reveals that the Civil Guard is investigating the Lionel Messi Foundation's financial records in the belief that some of the proceeds of charity matches may have ended up in some of the footballer's offshore accounts. Separately, there are fresh allegations that the matches may have been used by drug traffickers to launder drug money – although there is no suggestion that the Barcelona player or his teammates who participated had any knowledge of this. And as if that's not enough, various NGOs claim they never received the charitable donations they were promised.

Chapter 9

Neymar's arrival

It's 2 August 2013, the day of the annual Joan Gamper Trophy. Despite the stifling heat, 81,000 Blaugrana fans have turned out to see what the team has in store for the forthcoming season. They will go home happy and confident of a great year ahead, or at least, it seems likely after Barcelona's resounding 8-0 defeat of visitors Santos.

Leo Messi is the first to score, and the victory is more or less theirs within half an hour. Neymar comes on in the second half and watches, amazed, as a spectator invades the pitch to give him a hug before being detained by four security guards. It is Ney's first match at the Nou Camp as Barça's newest signing. He is wearing number 11 and receives a standing ovation as he comes on. He is playing on the left wing, marked by Arouca, and his playing time overlaps with Messi for fifteen minutes. He is content to play it safe today, and seems more interested in passing the ball than in shooting. He avoids tricks and flourishes and instead serves up the perfect assist for the sixth goal, scored by Cesc Fàbregas. Towards the end of the goal-fest he has the opportunity to score, but he hits the crossbar.

'It's a strange feeling,' he says after the match. 'I'm happy that I can enjoy the victory with my team and new teammates. But I'm also sad for my friends from Santos, whom I love very much.'

Ney had arrived in the Catalan capital on the morning of 28 July. The following day he meets his new teammates. Next up it's the medical, followed by his first training session in the Ciutat Esportiva with Messi and Co. At the end of the session, he tweets: 'My dreams have come true. Thank you Lord!'

On 30 July he is already on a plane to Poland for a friendly against Lechia Gdańsk. He starts on the bench and comes on for Alexis Sánchez in the 78th minute, by which time Messi has already been substituted. Ney's Barcelona debut consists of twelve minutes in a match that ends 2-2. Not so exciting, granted, but it's enough to put a smile on his face.

'Barcelona is much better than I thought. It is a great feeling,' he says. 'I am very happy to be able to speak to Messi, to be near Xavi and Iniesta.' He adds that he is working to adapt as quickly as possible to Barça's style of play, which he considers 'the best in the world'. After that comes the aforementioned Joan Gamper Trophy, his first chance to play at the Nou Camp – and with Messi.

Meanwhile, Brazil is mourning the loss of one of

its great up-and-coming players. The Brazilians are also up in arms because Barcelona have reportedly told Ney to put on three kilos to adapt to European football.

'It could be a disaster. He could lose his qualities as has happened to other players,' laments physical trainer for Santos, Ricardo Sosa. 'Sure, if you look at Neymar, you see he is thin and has no muscles but he is very, very strong. His legs are made for running, for dribbling and for skipping around other players. He is agile, quick and, unlike other strikers, he has incredible stamina. He never gets tired and can repeat moves, one, two, three, four, five times. He takes knocks from defenders. Yes, he goes down but he doesn't get seriously hurt. It would be a shame if they made him put on bulk and muscles.'

And Luiz Felipe Scolari – then national coach for Brazil – loses his patience when he hears that Barcelona have put the kid on a diet and supplements to boost his iron levels. 'It's as though they know everything over there and we are the third world and we do not know anything,' he says. 'When he eats like a horse at midday, at three in the afternoon, and six and nine, he is great. He is on form. If he wasn't, he wouldn't play the way he is playing for Barcelona.'

Thousands of miles away, the new signing is already earning his keep. He is largely responsible for Barça winning their first official title of the season: the

Spanish Supercup. In the first leg on 21 August, Atlético Madrid are up 1-0. Messi has had to go off at half-time with a muscle problem, and it seems as though Atlético are going to have an easy ride. Alexis and Mascherano are the only Barça players holding the fort. Neymar comes on for Pedro in the 59th minute. Seven minutes later, he puts Barcelona back in the game. Xavi passes to Dani Alves on the right, and Neymar moves to the back post. Juanfran doesn't realise he is behind him. Ney beats him to the ball and heads it in, and Courtois can't get there. It is the Brazilian's first goal in an official match. He hugs Alves and the others and heads over to the bench to coach Tata Martino and his teammates. The away goal is enough to clinch his first trophy with Barça, after the return leg at the Nou Camp finishes 0-0.

Eight matches later he scores his first Liga goal, against Real Sociedad on 24 September. It is not a pretty goal, rather it's the result of mistakes by the opposition's defence. Goalkeeper Claudio Bravo and central defender Liassine Cadamuro manage to turn an innocent-looking cross from Alexis into a scuffle over the line for the Blaugrana number 11. As Neymar says afterwards: 'The ball was crying when it crossed the line.' He dedicates it to his son, David Lucca, whom he had introduced to the fans before the match, just as Leo Messi had done with his son Thiago.

But it's on 1 October against Celtic in Glasgow that the Brazilian really begins to show his maturity. In Messi's absence, the new Barça number 11 takes the lead, playing a tight, decisive game, and putting on a valiant effort. The Blaugrana win thanks to a Cesc goal from a Neymar counter-attack, earning him praise from the entire dressing room.

He is on top form going into the first *Clásico* against Real Madrid, the match with the most stars – worth the most millions – on one pitch. Messi and Neymar versus Cristiano and Gareth Bale. It's 26 October, the tenth Liga matchday of the season. By 8.00pm the match is sewn up, and the Nou Camp spectators are on their feet applauding Neymar Júnior as he goes off. He has scored and provided an assist, and been a key factor in Barcelona's win.

In the nineteenth minute Iniesta passes from the edge of the area to Neymar on the left. The number 11 fires the ball hard along the ground and it goes straight between the legs of Caravajal and Varane, who deflects the ball ever so slightly, putting off goalkeeper Diego López. Goal! It is Neymar's first *Clásico* goal, and it puts Barça in the lead. He continues to impress on the counter-attack, providing an assist for the Wonderkid Alexis, who seals the victory with a stunning shot.

The following day, the global press are emphatic: Neymar has been the star of the night. No one in the

Barça camp can hide their delight that he has adapted to the club's style so well. He still needs to iron out a few details, but he has been a breath of fresh air and has provided the missing piece of the puzzle while Messi is out injured.

But overnight things turn sour when Jordi Cases rattles the cages and goes public with his allegations about Barça over Ney's signing. In the weeks that follow, he will endure a level of media pressure that few footballers have ever experienced – much less at the tender age of 21. Even his first hat-trick in a Barça shirt – three goals in just fourteen minutes against Celtic in the Champions League on 11 December – will be overshadowed by the controversy.

On 16 January 2014 Barça play a Copa del Rey return-leg match against Getafe. It is only the third time since the start of the season that Neymar and Messi have been on the pitch together. The game ends 2-0 to the Blaugrana (6-0 on aggregate), but the Brazilian is left with a sprained right ankle and will be out for a month. Just when Leo had returned from two months out, now it's Juninho's turn to take a break. Barcelona are still top of La Liga.

One month later Neymar is back on the pitch as Barcelona quash Rayo at the Nou Camp with a resounding 6-0 win. He scores the sixth, finishing a spectacular play four minutes before the final whistle. The goal deserves a decent celebration, and he goes over to dance in front of the crowd with good friend Dani Alves, breaking out moves inspired by a recent hit song from the Brazilian carnival. But once again he finds himself in the eye of the storm, as some pundits think such a celebration is disrespectful to the opponents after such a humiliating defeat.

It is to be an annus horribilis for Barcelona. On 23 February they lose their Liga lead after being crushed 3-1 by Real Sociedad at Anoeta Stadium. Neymar's performance is barely worthy of note – his mind seems somewhere else. The press and the fans are not hiding their disappointment in the Ney-Messi partnership. They have barely been on the same pitch together due to various injuries, and when they have, there has been almost no chemistry. The *Clásico* at the start of the season seems a lifetime ago. In La Liga so far, the Brazilian has not received a single assist from the Argentine, and the Argentine has received just three from Neymar, all back in September.

The next few weeks will be a tough time for the team, who are barely recognisable from the exquisite, trophy-hauling Barça of recent seasons. They suffer two significant blows on the pitch: they are knocked out of the Champions League in the quarter-finals by Atlético Madrid (2-1 on aggregate), and they lose the final of the Copa del Rey 2-1 to Real Madrid at Mestalla. Neymar is injured in that last match, this time suffering a contusion in his left foot.

Three weeks later, once he has recovered, he is in the squad for the most important match of the year: the final Liga clash of the season against Atlético Madrid. Barça have to win if they want to take home the trophy, but the best they can manage is a 1-1 draw. The Brazilian only comes on for Pedro in the last half hour, in time to watch his team close out their worst season in many years.

He has played in 53 matches, scored fourteen goals and made eight assists. To be fair, all too often Tata has put him on the right rather than the left where he is more comfortable – and the centre of the attack is, of course, Messi's domain. But that's not the only reason. He also misses Brazil, and the controversy surrounding his transfer must surely have had an effect on him, although he has never let it show in public. He's an elite sportsman, but criticism is criticism, and he has endured plenty in recent months.

One of the toughest blows came towards the end of March from ex-Barça coach Johan Cruyff, who had been a vocal opponent of Rosell's tenure. 'Barcelona have created a problem: they have signed a 21-year-old who earns more than everyone else and who has already got it all,' claimed the Dutchman. 'Everyone has to learn at 21 – there is no such thing as a 21-year-old god.'

Looking ahead to the 2014-15 season, Neymar now has to find his place under a new coach, the Spaniard

Luis Enrique. But things are looking up, with the partnership with Messi working well during the opening matches. They are working together more closely and seem to have a greater understanding. In the third match of the season, against Athletic Bilbao, the Brazilian is responsible for both goals, thanks to assists from the Argentine. Ney hasn't been playing for as many minutes in each match as he did the previous year, but he is shooting more, and scoring more goals – including three on 27 September in Barça's 6-0 whitewash of Granada.

Perhaps it's a good omen. At least he has the whole season ahead to prove himself.

Chapter 10

World Cup

Three, two, one ... that's how many World Cups Messi, Suárez and Neymar have played, respectively. All three are the big stars of their national teams, carrying the pride and hopes of their nations on their shoulders. And they all have stars on their shirts denoting previous wins: five for the Brazilian, two apiece for the Argentine and the Uruguayan. But they have merely inherited those stars. To be part of the winning team is still a pipe dream for them. The World Cup is a bittersweet experience. It represents unfinished business.

Germany 2006

Ever the early bird, Leo makes his World Cup debut at just eighteen years of age. The fans have included him on a six-strong shortlist from which they will vote for the young player of the tournament. The Argentines want to see Messi in the starting line-up and they have pinned all their hopes on him. They want evidence of all the amazing stories that are told across Europe about the heir to Maradona – and they want it in the shape of a national shirt.

The Albiceleste is in Group C, known from the beginning as the group of death: Ivory Coast, Serbia and Montenegro, and the Netherlands. It will not be an easy ride, especially with the disaster of 2002's South Korea and Japan World Cup weighing on their minds. Saturday 10 June at 9.00pm in Hamburg sees the first match against the Ivory Coast. During a training session five days earlier, Messi suffered a contusion, making it difficult for him to play. Coach José Pekerman's plan is to pace him, allowing him to go on later in the competition, apart from anything because they are not convinced he is 100 per cent fit.

From the bench, Lionel watches as Crespo scores his 30th international goal in typical opportunist fashion. He watches as Riquelme, in a moment of divine inspiration, looks into the stands and sends the ball exactly where it needs to go. And he sees the unmarked 'Conejo' Saviola punish Tizié with his first touch. He watches as the Ivory Coast's Elephants fight back and try to create chances without getting a goal – they only manage it towards the end, thanks to Drogba as usual, breaking through the Argentine defence, led by the impeccable Ayala. The result: 2-1. The Albiceleste look promising, even without Leo.

On 16 June against Serbia and Montenegro at the Gelsenkirchen stadium, Pekerman has no intention of fixing what isn't broken. In short, Messi is starting on the bench again. He has Carlos Tévez, the other youngster on the team, to keep him company, and 65 minutes to witness three goals and wonder how many he could score. Then he is on his feet, in his fluorescent outfit, warming up along the touchline. The warm-up is a promising sign. He returns to the dugout, following gestures and instructions, and finally assistant coach Hugo Tocalli lets him put on the blue number 19 shirt. His World Cup debut comes in the 74th minute. He comes on for Maxi Rodríguez, joining the game at the same time as Tévez.

In the stands, Maradona lifts his arms in the air, screaming and cheering along with the thousands of Argentine fans. They sing: 'Olé, olé olé olé, Me-ssiiiii, Me-ssiiiii!' Someone holds up a poster with the Flea's face next to the World Cup trophy. Underneath it says: 'This is my dream.'

The Flea's appearance stirs the team, who seem to be in a bit of a rut. They pass him the ball and he's off like a shot, with the sole objective of making it to the opponents' goal. He creates quite a spectacle as he skips along. A free kick is taken quickly and Leo is onto it, zooming along on the left-hand side of the penalty area. He reaches the line, lifts his head and slides the ball in front of the goalposts in a perfect position for Crespo who, anticipating the Serbian defence, stretches out his foot and takes the total number of goals to four. In the 87th minute Tévez passes to Crespo, who passes back to Tévez who, after having scored the fifth goal, shows his generosity by sending the ball down to Messi, who is motoring up the right wing. He gets past the defender and scores the sixth goal, sliding the ball between the post and the goalkeeper's hand. Then he pauses to point to the player who gifted him the goal. Crespo rushes over to hug him as the crowd goes wild. It is impossible to imagine a more stunning debut.

In the following match against the Netherlands on 21 June, Pekerman has no qualms about promoting him to the starting line-up. But it's not his night. His presence on the pitch is barely felt and the coach substitutes him for Julio Cruz in the 69th minute. It had been the most highly anticipated match of the first stage of the World Cup, a clash between two powerful teams with many great precedents (the 1978 final in particular), but it ended up being disappointing. Some journalists maliciously imply that the number 19's rather ordinary performance will give Pekerman the perfect excuse to put him back on the bench. And back he goes.

On 24 June, his nineteenth birthday, he is back to being a spectator for 84 long minutes. And this time Argentina are not doing well: Mexico, coached by the Argentine Ricardo La Volpe, have got them against the ropes. When Messi comes on for Saviola, the score is 1-1. The game is heading into extra time. And it is then that the boy from Barça changes the team's rhythm: he gives it the necessary depth and sends the ball from foot to foot, building up to an amazing Maxi Rodríguez goal. Albeit with more difficulties than anticipated, Argentina have made it into the quarter-finals.

In Berlin, on 30 June, they face host team Germany. There are 120 minutes of play, of which Leo Messi plays not even a single minute. It is a mystery, the polemic of a match that ends with Argentina losing on penalties (4-2, after a 1-1 score at the end of extra time).

South Africa 2010

In 2010 Messi has another opportunity to demonstrate that he can achieve the same sort of glory with the Albiceleste as he does with Barça. This time, it's Diego Armando Maradona in the dugout. Maradona-Messi, Messi-Maradona ... the relationship appears to have found stability after all the back and forth, all the criticism and contradictory statements, and all the references to the Oedipus complex.

The first match is on 12 June at Ellis Park stadium in Johannesburg. Lionel lights up the Albiceleste's game, he understands the needs of the team and he is the most active member of the Argentine attack. He does everything: he plays in the hole, he's on the wing, he's a striker, he puts in crosses. At the end of the match, won by a header from Gabriel Heinze, Maradona rushes over to Messi and lifts him up in his arms. 'Messi was on the ball all day. When he has the ball he has fun, and while he's having fun he entertains us all,' Diego remarks at the press conference later, while munching on an apple.

And the show continues. Against South Korea Messi excels in the hole, up front, and as general playmaker. The Flea organises the game, he gets the ball moving, he takes the free kicks and corners, and he gifts stunning passes to the strikers. He has a hand in each of Argentina's four goals. He takes the free kick which Park Chu-Young puts in his own net; he crosses for 'Pipita' Higuaín's first goal; then he zigzags between the Korean defenders, shoots, Jung blocks the goal with his foot, his second attempt is just wide of the post but Pipita picks it up for his second goal. And to finish it off, he sets up the perfect assist for Kun, who then gives Pipita his hat-trick – scored right in front of the tournament organisers. Argentina goes from being condemned to ridicule to being one of the favourites.

On 22 June against Greece, Leo goes out onto the pitch wearing the captain's armband. It's the first time he has led his national team. After a tough match hampered by the cold at the Peter Mokaba stadium in Polokwane, Argentina beat Greece 2-0 and claim their place in the last sixteen with three group stage victories.

Five days later, they defeat Mexico 3-1 with minimal effort. Messi loses his bet with Maradona – he doesn't score a single goal. 'I have to score two against Germany or that's it,' jokes the number 10 at the end of the match. But he won't even come close. In the quarter-final, Joachim Löw's team flatten the Albiceleste with a humiliating 4-0 victory. Maradona's tactical gamble, which had been hailed as revolutionary, fails Messi again and again, just when it matters most. It is fifteen minutes before he even touches the ball. Stuck far away from the goal, Lionel loses the ball twelve times and doesn't manage to get it back. He is despairing over the fact that on the few occasions when he does manage to break free from the Germans, his teammates don't manage to feed him the ball. He is left in no man's land, foundering fast.

His World Cup score sheet is dismal. He has played five matches, he has taken more shots than anyone – 30 times, twelve on target and two off the post – but he has had no luck. He bows out of the World Cup without a single goal to his name, unable to contain his tears.

*   *   *

Over in the Uruguay camp, Luis Suárez is having a much better tournament. At the start, the Celeste are in the group of death, up against host nation South Africa, previous runners-up France, and Mexico, who are always a tough nut to crack.

Their first match is against France on 11 June at Green Point stadium, Cape Town. Suárez is sporting number 9, up front with Diego Forlán as part of Tabárez's 4-4-2 formation. Suárez plays until the 72nd minute, when he is substituted by Sebastián 'Loco' Abreu. He has made his mark on the game with a knock-on to Forlán – despite pressure from Gallas – and the shot goes wide. The match flatlines, ending 0-0.

On 16 June in Pretoria, South Africa come out onto the pitch hoping to live up to the Springboks, their national rugby team who won the World Cup in 1995 and 2007. But it's not to be. Forlán scores the first two, and Álvaro Pereira makes it 3-0, as the Celeste shatter the dreams of a nation that had been preparing for this special tournament. Luis is on fire, putting on a fantastic performance, but he doesn't manage to score.

For that he will have to wait until the Mexico game on 22 June, when he scores his first World Cup goal in the 42nd minute. Pereira retrieves the ball for Uruguay in their half and passes to Forlán in the centre circle. Diego turns to see where his team are. In a flash, he passes to Cavani who has run up the right flank, while Suárez is getting into position on the left.

A perfect cross from Edinson, Luis frees himself from his markers and with a clean header the ball careers into the back of the net: 1-0. It's a goal that will take Uruguay into the final sixteen.

On to a rainy Port Elizabeth, where Lucho puts on a masterful performance against South Korea, making it 1-0 after just eight minutes. Their opponents manage to equalise, but Luis scores again in the 80th minute, taking the Celeste into the quarter-finals. He receives the ball on the edge of the area, perfect ball control, darts to the right to break free, then a quick glance and, bam – the ball flies through the air and slams into the opposite corner of the goal. The number 9 is off, running like a madman, jumping over the fence at the edge of the pitch, going over to hug the subs. Uruguay haven't made it this far since 1970.

2 July 2010, Johannesburg, Soccer City: Ghana vs Uruguay. The Black Stars are the last African team left in play. No one could have imagined that this would be the most dramatic game of the tournament. The scoreline is stuck at 1-1 after extra time, with goals by Muntari and Forlán. In the dying seconds of injury time, Portuguese referee Olegário Benquerença blows for a foul by Jorge Fucile on Adiyiah. The Uruguayans protest vehemently, saying Fucile did not even touch his opponent. But the free kick is given. Pansil takes it, and the ball loops into the area. Chaos ensues, with headers and jostling and players bundled to

the ground. The ball is tapped off the line and then Adiyiah heads for goal. Muslera is beaten and Suárez, who is the last man on the line, perhaps remembering how uncle 'El Chango' Suárez used to put him in goal, somehow parries the ball with both hands and gets himself sent off. He stands on the sideline, shirt over his head, unable to watch. Gyan steps up to take the penalty, and stares down the barrel of destiny. He takes a long run up, and slams the ball into the crossbar. The final whistle blows – the match will be decided on penalties.

In the end it goes Uruguay's way. It doesn't matter what the rest of the world thinks: Lucho's handball has made him a national hero. On 6 June he has to watch from the stands as the Celeste are knocked out of the semis 3-1 by the Netherlands. And a few days later they are beaten 3-2 by Germany in the race for third place. But it hardly matters. Fourth place is still reason enough for Uruguay to celebrate.

Brazil 2014

If El Pistolero's handball in South Africa caused a stir, it was nothing compared with the controversy that will sully his name in Brazil.

He arrives at the tournament with a knee injury and stays on the bench for the first match against Costa Rica in Fortaleza on 14 June, enduring the Celeste's defeat from the sidelines. The match had started well, with a penalty from Cavani. But Joel Campbell equalises with a powerful left-footed shot, and Oscar Duarte heads in the second to make it 2-1. Marcos Ureña scores right on the whistle to make it 3-1 to Costa Rica at the close.

Things couldn't be off to a worse start. Tabárez knows he has missed out on three crucial points to help them through to the final sixteen. They will have to go all out against England. 'We need to get back on track with our weapons at the ready,' he says. And one of his weapons is Suárez.

That's exactly what happens on 19 June in São Paulo. Nicolás Lodeiro gets things going with a counter-attack on the left with Cavani, who waits before releasing the perfect cross to Lucho, who heads the ball past England goalie Joe Hart to make it 1-0. El Pistolero shoots his finger guns in the air, laughing. He runs to the bench to hug physio Walter 'El Manosanta' Ferreira, pointing at him wildly. Without him, Suárez would not have been fit to play. Ferreira is battling cancer and had been alternating his chemotherapy with Luis's physio sessions. He had not known right up until the last moment whether he would be able to travel to Brazil, but he had made the impossible possible.

In the 75th minute Wayne Rooney brings the scores level. But the Three Lions' reprieve is short-lived. With seven minutes to go, Suárez finishes them off thanks to a long pass from Muslera, which Steven Gerrard (of all people) deflects into Luis's path. The Uruguayan does not need asking twice. He hustles past Cahill and makes what can only be described as an immaculate finish. A cannonball which Hart does not even see. A few minutes later he comes off, due to the cramp that had set in twenty minutes earlier.

Only the match against Italy stands between Uruguay and the final sixteen. Natal, 24 June, a date that will go down in footballing history. The Blues only need a draw. The Celeste have to win to go through. It's 0-0 at 78 minutes. The Italians are a man down after Claudio Marchisio's sending off. Uruguay are giving it their all, but Suárez missed a clear chance in the 65th minute. He is hanging around in the box, trying to wait out the final minutes. And that's when it happens.

The ball is in the air and is launched back upfield but ends up with Stuani in the area. Cavani appears on the left. Buffon has already raised his hand in the box. There are two players on the floor. What is going on? Suárez is holding his teeth and looks to be in pain. Chiellini is holding his arm and calling the ref. What the hell is going on? The replay shows the Uruguayan number 9 running towards Chiellini waiting for a cross and then running into the Juventus defender's shoulder. Chiellini reacts with an elbow in Suárez's face.

At first it looks like a head butt. But then it

becomes clear that El Pistolero has bitten his opponent. Chiellini is yelling in Spanish. He pulls his shirt down and indicates that he has been bitten on his left shoulder. But the ref hasn't seen the incident and play continues.

In the 81st minute Italy crumble and Diego Godín takes advantage of the corner to feed Buffon the goal. Uruguay are through.

But Luis is not. The next few days will be the most difficult of his life. It's not the first time he has bitten someone, but now he has done it in front of an international audience. FIFA expel him from the tournament and he leaves Brazil in tears. Two days later his teammates follow him after losing 2-0 to Colombia.

* * *

Neymar has also had an abrupt exit from the tournament. 'I could have ended up in a wheelchair,' he says at a press conference six days after the injury that put him out of the World Cup – 'his' World Cup. He has fractured his third vertebra, and it is revealed that if Colombian Juan Camilo Zúñiga had hit him 'two centimetres closer to the middle', he would not have been able to walk.

His pain is that of a nation that dreamt of bringing home its sixth World Cup, after triumphs in Sweden in 1958, Chile in 1962, Mexico in 1970, the United States in 1994 and Japan and South Korea in 2002.

Not winning was not an option for the Brazilians. It's a tale of failure and collective disappointment, and it's as difficult to get over as the 'Maracanazo' – as Brazil's 2-1 defeat by Uruguay in the 1950 final is famously known. The World Cup is over, and there have been no sparks of brilliance or ingenuity from the host nation.

The Canaries' first match against Croatia on 12 June opens with an own goal in the eleventh minute. But they recover as quickly as possible and Neymar manages to equalise. In the 78th minute Yuichi Nishimura awards a penalty for an apparent foul on Fred, something nobody but the Japanese referee seems to have seen. And Ney takes a left-footed shot to put his team in the lead. Finally in injury time, Óscar seals a 3-1 win. A first victory for the home team, albeit a rather lacklustre one – no strokes of genius, no charisma, and a little too much controversy. Only one player seems to be up to the sort of standard expected of the only team in the world to have played in every World Cup: Neymar Júnior. The number 10 is crowned man of the match, and describes his feelings with a single word: 'happy'.

Everyone's worst fears are confirmed on 17 June: this Brazil team is a shadow of its former self. Against Mexico in the second Group A match they can only manage a 0-0 draw. There is no trace of the team who won the FIFA Confederations Cup just a year earlier, and their place in the last sixteen hangs in the balance. The Mexicans are hungry, and more importantly they have 'Memo' Ochoa, a goalkeeper in the midst of one of the performances of his career. His incredibly quick reflexes enable him to block three dangerous chances: one from Paulinho in the 43rd minute, one from Neymar in the 68th, and a shot by captain Thiago Silva after a cross from the number 10 in the 86th. Apart from that, Brazil muster little else to excite the 60,000 spectators in the packed stadium or the millions watching across the globe.

Monday 23 June, Mané Garrincha National Stadium, Brasilia. 'This was definitely our best match – not just because of the result, but because of our whole performance. The way we kept up the pressure on our opponents was crucial. We won comfortably and we deserved to. We are on the right path and we will keep improving every day.' Neymar is ecstatic: his team are through to the last sixteen after beating Cameroon 4-1 in the final group match. The young footballer can go home with his head held high, in the knowledge that were it not for his talent and thirst for victory, it could have been an entirely different story. Because, despite the number 10's generous comments, the result is rather deceiving. Their star player aside, Brazil still have a lot of problems to iron out. The host team have been entirely dependent on the Barcelona forward.

Five days later, the Canaries are crying tears of anguish, then joy. The tense final-sixteen match against Chile is the backdrop for some of the most surreal images of this World Cup. It's one goal apiece: in the eighteenth minute David Luiz nets one for Brazil after a corner. And in the 32nd Eduardo Vargas scores for Chile. The match goes to penalties. And this is where the 33 cameras at the Mineirão capture an alarming scene. Júlio César crying. Captain Thiago Silva refusing to take a shot and going to pray in the corner of the pitch. Brazil are paralysed with fear. Even Neymar drops to his knees before getting ready to take his shot. 'I felt like I was running three kilometres rather than three steps,' he would say later, 'but the most difficult part was when I got to the ball and had to shoot.' Luck is on the Brazilians' side – the shootout ends 3-2 in their favour, and practically the entire team breaks down in tears, as if in a collective catharsis.

And so we arrive at the fateful Friday 4 July 2014. Everything is going well, Ney's team have already done enough to go through to the semis, when Juan Camilo Zúñiga knees him in the back. He falls face down on the ground, screaming in pain, holding his back. Marcelo runs over to him and the Barça forward tells him he can't feel his legs. The whole team fear the worst. His pain is all too visible as he is rushed off on a stretcher. A few hours later the doctors confirm the fracture to his third vertebra, an incredibly rare injury in football and one that will keep him out for three to six weeks. Neymar's World Cup is over. The Colombia match – the best the team has played all tournament – is to be his last. It ends 2-1 to Brazil.

Without the kid from Mogi, the team suffer a humiliating 7-1 defeat at the hands of Germany in the semis. Eight days later, they are back on the pitch to face the Netherlands in the third place play-offs. Neymar watches from the dugout as they lose 3-0. He is the only one spared the boos of the crowd.

* * *

And what about Messi? The 2014 World Cup is also a disappointment for the Flea. He is within reach of realising his dream of becoming world champion, but Germany bring him back to earth with a bump. The *Mannschaft* are longstanding rivals of the Argentines and they certainly know how to crush their dreams. The last time the two teams faced each other in the final was in Italy in 1990, and the Germans waited until the last possible moment to clinch the trophy on that occasion too, with a controversial penalty, converted by Andreas Brehme in the 86th minute. It was revenge as much as anything. Four years earlier in Mexico it had been Argentina who had claimed their second World Cup – against who else but Germany. That was Diego Armando Maradona's World Cup, just as 2014 had been touted as Lionel Messi's World Cup.

The Barcelona player has been carrying the hopes and dreams of an anxious country on his shoulders, but Brazil has not gone as Leo had hoped. For someone who always wins, coming second is a bitter failure. His only consolation is winning the Golden Ball for player of the tournament.

There is plenty of debate about whether he deserves it, but there is no doubt that he has been decisive during the Albiceleste's first four matches. And coach Alejandro Sabella has certainly built his team around his number 10. He has not been on his best form in Spain, but now that he is back on his home continent he hopes to turn things around. Unlike in previous years, no one is in any doubt about his 'Argentine-ness' and his loyalty to his national team. He is now their revered captain and everything is built around him.

Argentina's first match is on 15 June against Bosnia Herzegovina, their most dangerous Group F rival, who will make them sweat it out for their first victory, despite putting them ahead with an own goal in the third minute. The Albiceleste look uncomfortable, and the fact that they are one of the favourites doesn't seem to bother their opponents. Bosnia are taking better advantage of their possession, until finally Messi decides enough is enough. The number 10 steals the ball, pushes the play forward with Higuaín and dodges past two defenders to make it 2-0 in the 65th minute and banish all thoughts of South Africa once and for all. There is nothing shy about his celebration, as he screams with joy and runs towards the corner flag to dedicate his goal to the fans. Just before the final whistle, Vedad Ibišević scores for Bosnia, but it's not enough to deny Argentina their three points. Mission accomplished, although the Albiceleste players have their doubts.

Next up, Iran. No one is expecting what follows: a tortuous match for the Albiceleste, and a lesson in courage by the Iranians. Argentina dominate the possession from the start, but they are unable to break through their opponents' defensive line. Iran, for their part, manage a couple of attempts on Sergio Romero's goal. But Messi seems impassive, the match is boring, and even Maradona, watching from the stands, decides to leave before the final whistle. Leo perks up for long enough to score one good goal and make it 1-0 at the close.

On 24 June Leo celebrates his 27th birthday with Antonella and Thiago. Twenty-four hours later, with their place in the last sixteen already sealed, Argentina face Nigeria. The Albiceleste put on a better performance than in their first two matches, moving more quickly and passing the ball a lot more freely. With his team playing well, Messi is on fire. He seems a lot more inspired and scores two beautiful goals, the first in the third minute and the second on the stroke of half-time. At 3-2 and with things already sewn up, Sabella decides to rest his number 10 in preparation for the knockout stages. The cameras zoom in to gauge Leo's reaction, but he comes off without a complaint, and is even smiling.

In the final sixteen they are up against Switzerland. The fans are looking forward to what they are sure will be another masterful lesson in footballing excellence, but they will be bitterly disappointed. Argentina win, but it's a struggle. Sabella's men seem inert, out of ideas. With the score still at 0-0 after 90 minutes, the match goes to extra time. Messi looks worn out, and takes the opportunity to put his feet up during the break. In the 118th minute he initiates a move, sees Ángel Di María to his right, and serves up the ball for the winning goal. It's the latest that Argentina have scored a winner in a World Cup, but it's enough to send them through to the quarter-finals – the 'cursed' round that has been their downfall since their last final at Italia '90.

On Saturday 5 July at the Mané Garrincha National Stadium in Brasília they are up against Belgium – a well organised team with strong players. But this time they are up to the challenge. Before even ten minutes have passed, Higuaín scores what will be his only goal of the tournament.

The Albiceleste are through to the semi-finals for the first time in 24 years. They are facing the

Netherlands, just two days after the death of Alfredo Di Stéfano, the Argentine football legend who immigrated to Spain like Messi. They are all too aware of what a historic moment they are about to experience. But the match on 9 July at the Arena de São Paulo ends with neither pain nor glory. Instead, it goes to penalties. Ron Vlaar is first up for the Netherlands ... and Romero clears it. Next it's Messi's turn, and he sends the ball zooming into Jasper Cillessen's net. The Flea has taken the first step towards the final, and the rest of the team follow his lead.

It's an Argentina vs Germany final – the most frequent final in history. When the big day comes, Messi plays an uneven game, and although he shoots a handful of times, it's Higuaín who really deserves the goal. Nonetheless, the Flea keeps the fans' hopes alive for almost 120 minutes, until, just when everyone thought they had it sewn up, a surprise goal from Mario Götze takes them to defeat.

Leo's performance is reminiscent of the recent 2013-14 season with Barça – a few flashes of brilliance, but no real magic. After such a promising start to the 2014 World Cup, Messi leaves Brazil empty-handed. His crestfallen expression as he goes up to collect the Golden Ball says it all.

Chapter 11

Global icons

Cue the rock music. In the dressing room, a man is visible from behind, getting ready. Black trousers, studded belt, worn boots, leather jacket. He grabs an electric guitar and puts on aviator sunglasses before heading out. It's Luis Suárez, and the crowd chants his name. The music playing in the background is 'Born to be Wild'. Fade to black, followed by the Pepsi logo.

This TV advert is just one example of how the Uruguayan has become a big money-maker. Just like Messi and Ney. They are global icons and ambassadors for a slew of brands. They have converted their personality and achievements on the pitch into a product that can be exported to the furthest corners of the world, reaching a global audience. They are extremely bankable, selling and promoting everything imaginable, from sportswear, banks, gambling sites, videogames and soft drinks to mobile phones, sweets, comics, TVs, sunglasses and fragrances ... the list is practically endless – and so are the profits.

Nowadays, income generated from publicity

appearances represents a significant percentage of an elite footballer's salary. In fact, rarely a week goes by in which Leo and the rest of his Blaugrana teammates aren't attending some event or presentation. And when they're not doing that, they are filming a campaign or posing for a photo shoot. Sometimes they don't even have to leave the training ground: it's enough for them just to show off the latest trainers that their sponsors have designed especially for them, the TV cameras zoom in for a close-up, and it makes the headlines.

They are natural-born sellers, although each one has his own style and approach. In the publicity stakes, just as on the pitch, you have to stand out, be unique and special. The objective is the same: score more than your rivals – or rather, sell more. And in order to pull it off you have to play a role, have something of that 'je ne sais quoi' that others are lacking, show some attitude on the pitch, and own it.

* * *

In this parallel footballing world, Neymar occupies one of the top spots. He is the second most marketable footballer after Real Madrid's Cristiano Ronaldo, coming in above Lionel. It's true that in recent years the Brazilian has fallen a few places in the annual ranking of all sportsmen published by Sports Pro magazine. In 2013 he was top, but now he has dropped down to seventh place. This is undoubtedly related to the big controversy surrounding his Barcelona signing, and the fact that his performance during his first season with the Blaugrana has not been as brilliant as expected.

Nonetheless, his face was one of the most utilised for marketing by every conceivable brand during the 2014 Brazil World Cup. In a five minute clip for the Beats by Dre headphones, Ney stars alongside his father, with other football stars, including Luis Suárez, playing supporting roles. It helps that it's a product that fits with the kid from Mogi's young, modern image. Neymar is synonymous with fun, daring and life in the fast lane. He's a charismatic, likeable kid, with his penchant for quirky hairstyles and tattoos, and his love of technology, music and fashion.

He has so many different advertising contracts that at times he blurs the line between publicity and reality. He makes headlines following the Champions League quarter-final against Atlético Madrid on 1 April 2014 – not just for scoring Barcelona's only goal, but for seemingly brandishing his underwear. Critics claim he is guilty of advertising, as every time he lifted his shirt or adjusted his shorts the logo of his longstanding underwear sponsor was clearly visible. The Brazilian insists there is no underlying strategy behind his movements.

But it's not the first time the marketing king has

been accused of using tricks to promote his products or himself. And it happens again just a few days later, with his 'We are all monkeys' anti-racism campaign. At first it seems like a spontaneous post that goes viral. Someone throws a banana at Dani Alves during a match against Villarreal, and instead of showing his annoyance, the player calmly bites into it. Within minutes, Neymar – who is watching the match on television – has Instagrammed a picture of himself, his son and a banana, with the hashtags #somostodosmacacos #weareallmonkeys. The reaction is huge – even Italian Prime Minister Matteo Renzi gets in on the act. A few hours later the Brazilian media reveal that the whole stunt was dreamt up by the Barça number 11's publicists.

Neymar is a big fish on social media. He and his advisors have tapped into a whole range of platforms to boost his personal image and brand in a way that is instantaneous, cost effective and globally visible. The key to his success is sharing moments of his life outside of matches, training and public appearances. He is the fourth most popular footballer on Twitter, with more than 15 million followers – still a far cry from Cristiano Ronaldo's 30 million, but enough to demonstrate how influential he is at just 22 years of age. It can't hurt that he posts things constantly – he always has a story to tell or a face to pull. He tweets nine times a day on average, which is significantly more than other sporting celebrities. And barely a day goes by without him posting photos to Instagram – with his friends, his father, his son, his teammates, sticking out his tongue, playing the piano or jumping on the bed.

* * *

If Neymar is the face of youthfulness, Leo symbolises authenticity. A big part of his attraction is the image of a normal kid who likes spending time with his family, friends and loved ones. Paradoxically, his shy nature makes him seem more accessible.

But it's more than that. From early on in his professional career, the image of Messi was that of a boy who succeeded in reaching the top despite his height and growth problems. With hard work, perseverance and strong will, he has demonstrated and continues to demonstrate to the wider world that nothing is impossible.

It's true that he doesn't have the same level of self-assurance in front of the cameras as Ney or even Suárez. Nonetheless, the promo he shot with basketball superstar Kobe Bryant for Turkish Airlines in 2012 has garnered more than 105 million views on YouTube. They followed it up in 2013 with a Kobe versus Messi 'Selfie Shootout', where the two compete to see who can take the most pictures of themselves in different locations – which got more than 130 million views.

But it's not just YouTube views that confirm Messi's status as a successful ambassador. According to France Football's 2014 'Salaries of the stars' report, the Barça player has raked in 26 million euros in advertising contracts. He is first on the top twenty list, ahead of Cristiano (22 million) and Neymar (14 million). It seems any past allegations of supposed tax evasion have not affected his image.

These sorts of figures indicate that Leo's shyness has receded over the years – something that is also reflected in the evolution of his designer fashion choices, particularly as the face of Dolce & Gabbana. Each Ballon d'Or or Golden Boot gala is an opportunity for him to break out an even more outlandish suit or tuxedo: bold colours, floral tapestry, polka dots … the louder the better.

When it comes to social media, he has 70 million Facebook fans, second only to Cristiano. But to date he has no presence on Twitter, which is unusual for such a big star. There are plenty of accounts bearing his name and picture, but his family and friends have had to step in on more than one occasion to confirm that they are not official accounts. As his sister María Sol has tweeted in the past: 'A message from Leo! "Once again I would like to clarify that I do not have a Twitter account and I don't intend to create one for now. If I did, I would announce it via my Facebook page. I hope this clarifies things so that people don't get misled by any accounts that contain my name."'

But there is another Messi on Twitter: Matías Messi, Leo's brother. His tweets have caused quite a stir among football fans – for example, by asking why Real fans follow him if they dislike him so much. And although he clarified that he wasn't talking about all Whites fans, the debate was already underway. He also caused a commotion when he posted a picture comparing Leo and Cristiano's various titles dating back to 2009.

*   *   *

In contrast to his teammates, Luis Suárez is a bit of a novice when it comes to the world of branding and publicity. He does have a presence on social media, and he has plenty of followers, fans and 'Likes'. But he isn't as active online as Ney, and can go several days without posting anything on Twitter.

Nor does he enjoy as much exposure from endorsements and publicity, as confirmed by his earnings. During his final season at Liverpool, he netted more than £10 million, of which only around £2.5 million came from sponsorship.

On the other hand he is extremely good at exploiting his key character traits: he is a fighter – competitive and unpredictable. He has taken his weaknesses – such as his tendency to protest against referees – and turned them into marketable assets. He is capable of laughing at his flaws and mustering a smile for the world. And he is not a bad actor. He had no problem starring in Pepsi's 'Born to be Wild' clip – a cheeky nod to his wild side, but daring considering his record on the pitch.

Of course, not all brands are willing to take that kind of risk. Following the bite at the World Cup, Luis loses some of his headline sponsors, such as betting site 888poker. The company states on Twitter that it will not tolerate 'unsporting behaviour'.

And it also seems to cast doubts over his future with Adidas. For many years the sportswear brand has been one of the main FIFA sponsors, and there is a possibility that continuing to support El Pistolero could be perceived as a conflict of interest. In the end, Adidas opts to pull all the World Cup campaign adverts featuring Suárez, but retains its collaboration with him.

Nonetheless, one particular sponsorship deal seems unlikely to be in any jeopardy – that of Abitab, one of Uruguay's main payment service providers, which features Luis in its adverts. Firstly, despite his aggression towards Chiellini, El Salteño never ceased to be a hero in his home country. Secondly, the company has spent many years using the star's controversial nature to its advantage.

In July 2013 it surprised viewers with a fun and irreverent TV advert, beginning with a voiceover that explains: 'At Abitab, we have been searching for a current celebrity to represent us around the country. That's why we hired Luis Suárez.' The footballer is seen dressed as a typical office worker in a white shirt and red tie, sending up exactly the sort of behaviour for which he is famous on the pitch: overreacting when the coffee runs out, getting frustrated with the photocopier, diving on the ground when a colleague merely taps him on the shoulder, and being so competitive as to blow out the candles on a co-worker's birthday cake. Of course, to make up for it, the colleagues are shown talking to the camera about his versatility, his ability to adapt to any role, and how much the customers love him. It's classic Lucho.

Only time will tell whether he will be able to rival Messi and Neymar in the publicity stakes – particularly now that he has joined the best team of recent years.

Chapter 12

Secrets of success

'Luis is a kid who has always wanted to improve. He has always trained hard and put in extra time. Not like lots of players who make their excuses and head home as soon as training is over. At Nacional, he would stay behind and take free kicks or shoot volleys or practise how to get past the wall on a free kick. You would have to kick him out most days. If you didn't, he would have stayed there,' recalls Rubén Sosa.

Thousands of miles away, Neymar was doing the same. 'I remember, when he finished training he went to the staff office, and was told, "Hey kid, go and eat in the canteen with the rest of the players." But he didn't want to, he continued practising on his own,' says Gremetal coach Alcides Magri Júnior.

Messi was also strong willed, with that constant desire to improve. 'Everyone wants to be a footballer when they're a kid,' says his brother Rodrigo. 'But he knew how to stay faithful to his childhood passion and pursue his dream because his happiness was, and still is, tied up with football. I was a striker, but Leo had something I never had: he was so strong-willed, he has worked so hard and has made so many sacrifices to become who he is today.'

Hard work, a desire to improve and a willingness to learn ... Leo, Luis and Ney haven't made it to the top by chance. They have had to make sacrifices along the way, and invest many hours in training, practising new plays and passes that mark them out from the rest. Of course, they also have talent, a gift for the game, that innate ability that makes them special. But without hard work and perseverance, they would never have become the world's best footballers.

'Suárez is the kind of guy who fights for every ball for the entire 90 minutes, he clashes with his opponents, he falls, he gets up, he pushes forward into the box,' says Sosa. 'He's not the kind of forward who just waits there for a chance, waiting for the perfect assist. He is never still, he is always on the move. He's not necessarily the most superb player technically. He has decent ball control. But he really knows how to move the play up the pitch.'

Out of the three players, Lucho is perhaps the best example of someone who achieved his dream through pure determination. Because unlike Messi and Neymar, the Uruguayan didn't stand out from a young age as being extraordinarily talented with the football. Rather, he was noted for his tenacity. 'What I liked about Luis was his ability to learn,' says Ricardo

Perdomo. 'In just two years, he picked up the knowledge, ability, technique and skill that other kids had not or could not. He was always learning. Each training session was a chance to take in something new. He set himself targets and did his utmost to make sure he reached them. It was a personal challenge to make sure he headed the ball better, kicked the ball more cleanly, took shots with his weaker foot and executed free kicks better.'

But make no mistake, though they may have had innate abilities, Leo and Ney put in just as much hard work. The Flea in particular was small and fragile, and at first glance no one believed in his potential. How was he going to take on kids nearly double his size? With a huge amount of willpower. 'When you saw him you'd think: this kid can't play ball. He's a dwarf, he's too fragile, too small,' says Adrián Coria. 'But immediately you'd realise that he was born different, that he was a phenomenon and that he was going to be something impressive.'

In Neymar's case, he was at a physical disadvantage because he was so skinny. 'Look at how he is now. You can imagine what he was like six or seven years ago,' says Zito, who remembers what Ney was like when he brought him to Santos. 'He was pretty thin, but, thanks to the club's hard work, bit by bit he gained seven or eight kilos of muscle mass and a top-rate physique.'

All three have had to endure difficult periods

in their lives, experiences that few kids have to go through at that age. Leo left his country at just thirteen to follow his dream, while Lucho did it at nineteen. Juninho's move came a little later, but still at a time when most youngsters haven't decided what path their life will take.

Messi himself acknowledges that it was a difficult journey to becoming who he is today: 'All kids want to be footballers, but in order to make it you need to work hard and make a lot of sacrifices. And you have to go through some very tough times, like when I decided to stay in Barcelona … It was my decision. No one forced me to make it. My parents asked me many times what I wanted to do. I wanted to stay in the youth academy because I knew that that was my chance to be a footballer. I was very responsible from a very young age.'

They work hard to fulfil a dream, to improve, learn, progress, be the best in their town, then their club, then the world … and then to stay at the top. And all because of their passion for the game. That's what they have in common, that marks them out from the rest. They are crazy about the ball. They live to play, and go to sleep at night dreaming about their next goal.

'We wanted to become professional football players, we were glued to the TV when there was a match on, we saw the professional players being interviewed …' says Ney's old Portuguesa teammate Léo Baptistão.

Francisco 'Pancho' Ferraro coached Messi's Under-20 Argentine team to its fifth World Cup win. He has no doubt as to why the Argentine is the only footballer in history to have won four Ballon d'Or awards. 'Leo just loves to play – the football is his favourite toy. He has so much fun with it and he can control it like nobody else,' he says.

And as Sosa says about Suárez: 'For those of us who saw him grow up, who coached him, it's a wonderful surprise to see where he has ended up. But it bears repeating: he made it because he has an incredible passion for football. He lives for it, it's what makes him happy.'

Another factor in the success of Barça's numbers 9, 10 and 11 is being surrounded by family and friends who support them and keep them on the straight and narrow. In the case of Messi and Neymar, big decisions about their future were made with their respective families, who have done everything in their power to help them realise their dreams. Their fathers have become their closest confidants, advisors and representatives. 'I can't predict the future, but I know that my family will always be around me,' Ney has said on more than one occasion.

Suárez's case was a little different. His parents divorced while he was still a child, and it had a great impact on him. His mother worked several jobs in order to take care of him and his siblings. He had to grow up more quickly than the others, and find his own path. Fortunately, he has found in Sofia the stability that he previously lacked.

Without that level of support it is difficult for a young star to keep their feet on the ground and remain a consummate professional. There are countless examples of footballers who have thrown their career away due to their love of partying, alcohol or drugs. A sportsman's body is his livelihood, and it is crucial he look after it. It's something Leo knows all too well ... when Pep Guardiola arrived in the Blaugrana dugout, he was surprised by the Argentine's unhealthy diet, comprising mainly meat, pasta, pizza, strawberry ice cream and fizzy drinks. No fish, fruit or vegetables. The coach switched him to a more healthy regime, bringing an end to the string of injuries that had plagued the player up until that point. It's a similar story to when Suárez arrived in the Netherlands, and began to realise that becoming the best started with taking care of himself from the inside out. We are what we eat, as the saying goes.

But the real key to success, the characteristic that really distinguishes a great champion from the average footballer is a thirst for victory. The need to win, regardless of time, place, opponent or circumstance, is what has made Luis, Leo and Ney the best.

'He knows no limits. He reacts even in the most difficult situations football can put you in,' Martín

Lasarte says of Suárez. 'We would be losing and he would believe we could turn things around and win. He would be goalless but he would say he knew he could score. He never gave up or lowered his head. He feared nothing and no one.' And everyone who has ever worked with Lucho agrees: his greatest asset is his desire to win, and his insistence that victory is always within reach. 'There was only one thing that he could not stomach, and that was losing,' says Wilson Píriz. 'He also wanted to score in every game he played. When he did not score, he got really pissed off.'

Coria remembers a similar irrepressible impulse within Messi: 'He was 1.2m tall. He dazzled against central defenders of 1.8m. He made a huge impact. And he had a strong temperament – he was competitive, he liked to win. I have never seem him resign himself to any result. He wanted to win every game.'

There is one final quality, a bonus ingredient that has been noted by those who have worked with the Barça stars during their careers. 'As a coach, I see it like this: there are special players and there are good players,' says former Santos coach Muricy Ramalho. 'Neymar is in the first group. Apart from that, I believe that for a player to be different from the other players, he has to be a good person. And he is.'

And that includes not letting success and money change you, or make you think you are indispensable. 'Fame has not gone to Leo's head. He is the same guy he has always been, despite having no privacy,' says Cristina Cubero, journalist for daily Catalan newspaper *Mundo Deportivo* (Sports World), who has followed the Flea's career since the early days. 'For example, a while ago he was back in Rosario and out driving when a kid stopped him at a red light, asking for a photo. The nice thing to do would have been to roll down the window and let the kid take a picture on his phone. But no. Leo pulled over and got out for the photo.'

According to Píriz, Suárez is similarly big-hearted. 'He was level-headed, determined and hungry for success. He had a heart so big that it has made him into the man and footballer he is today. It is his big heart, his open nature, his easy-going attitude that won the hearts and minds of his teammates, his coaches and his managers.'

Chapter 13

Suárez's arrival: early days

Montevideo, 30 June 2014: 'After several days of being home with my family, I have had the opportunity to calm down and reflect about the reality of what occurred during the Italy-Uruguay match on 24 June 2014. Aside from the fallout and the contradicting statements that have surfaced during these past few days, all of which have been without the intention of interfering with the good performance of my national team, the reality is that my colleague, Giorgio Chiellini, suffered the physical result of a bite in the collision he suffered with me. For this, I deeply regret what happened. I apologise to Giorgio Chiellini and the entire footballing community. I vow to the public that there will never again be another incident like this.'

This is Luis Suárez's apology, the *mea culpa* everyone has been waiting for. The Uruguayan has done his bit, and now nothing stands in the way of him donning the number 9 shirt for Barça. It's hardly a surprise, it's what everyone assumed would happen.

'If he apologises, he signs,' claimed the front page of *Sport* on 27 June 2014, right after Suárez had received his ban. 'FC Barcelona waits for an admission of the player's mistake in order to finish negotiations.'

Three days after Lucho publishes his statement on his website, Barça sporting director Andoni Zubizarreta comments: 'He's shown enough strength and humility to recognise his mistake, to ask for forgiveness from Chiellini and football in general. That's the start of the recovery process of any person who's done something badly wrong. His current behaviour says a lot about him. Apologising is not an easy thing.' It's as though he is giving the signing his blessing.

It's a transfer that has been commented on at length, before Luis's actions against the Italian defender in the World Cup. In fact, it has been the topic of debate since before the tournament even began. And just as with Neymar the previous year, there is talk that Real Madrid are also interested in El Pistolero. Rumour has it that the Blaugrana and the Whites are preparing to vie for yet another superstar. Whether or not that's true, Real are quickly out of the picture. In the days that follow, the press claim he will go to Barcelona because, they say: 'His daughter was born there and he has relatives in Catalonia; Alexis Sánchez is being wooed by Liverpool, which could reduce the transfer fee; and new Blaugrana coach Luis Enrique likes him and may have already given his approval.'

The hype surrounding the new arrival is at its peak, although the bite causes a definite setback. Barça can't afford another controversial signing after the headache that is still ongoing following their purchase of Neymar. But Suárez's official apology is enough to smooth things over. Now it's just a matter of negotiations – price, payment method and possible exchanges of players. Obviously the Catalans will try to get a better price for the player since FIFA has rejected the Uruguayan Football Association's appeal and confirms that he will serve the full length of the ban. Not having Suárez in the team until the end of October is surely worth a bit of a discount.

On Friday 11 July, just after 1.00pm, FC Barcelona announce their deal to sign Luis Suárez from Liverpool FC on a five-year contract, for a lower salary than the £200,000 a week he was paid at the English club, and less than that of Messi, Neymar and Iniesta. According to the Catalan club the transfer fee is 81 million euros, making him the fourth most expensive player in the history of La Liga, and Barça's second highest after Neymar. The club will cover the cost with the sale of Alexis to Arsenal for 42.5 million, Cesc Fàbregas to Chelsea for 36 million and Jonathan dos Santos to Villarreal for 2 million.

Financial details aside, the mind boggles at the idea of an attacking line-up comprising Leo Messi, Neymar and Lucho. The trio scored 87 goals between them in the previous season. It remains to be seen how they will gel on the field, and they will have to wait until October, as El Pistolero will miss the start of La Liga and the first three matches of the 2014-15 Champions League.

But the main thing is that he has made it to Barça, his dream team for many years. Before leaving Liverpool, he writes an emotional farewell message on his website: 'It is with a heavy heart that I leave Liverpool for a new life and new challenges in Spain. Both my family and I have fallen in love with this club and with the city. But most of all I have fallen in love with these incredible fans. You have always supported me, and we as a family will never forget it, we will always be Liverpool supporters. I hope you all can understand why I have made this decision. This club did all they could to get me to stay, but playing and living in Spain, where my wife's family live, is a lifelong dream and ambition. I believe now the timing is right. I wish Brendan Rodgers and the team the best for the future. The club is in great hands and I'm sure will be successful again next season. I am very proud I have played my part in helping to return Liverpool to the elite of the Premier League and in particular back into the Champions League. Thank you again for some great moments and memories. You'll Never Walk Alone.'

Within a few days he has settled into a hotel in the

Catalan capital, near his in-laws' home. He is spending most of his time with Sofia and the kids, house hunting and finding schools, acclimatising, and doing some personal training with Barça head physio Juanjo Brau. He pushed himself a bit too much to be fit for the World Cup, and now he needs to recover. Reports in the press suggest that Brau is also instructing him in the important matter of 'Barcelonismo' – what it means to be part of a club that is 'more than just a club', and preparing him on how to fit in once his ban is over.

On 4 August FIFA's disciplinary committee confirms that he will miss the opening eight matches of La Liga. Three days later, he arrives in Switzerland with experts from Barça and the Uruguayan FA to try to convince the Court of Arbitration for Sport (CAS) that the sanctions are 'disproportionate and without precedent'.

At the very least, Barcelona want him to be able to train with his teammates, which he is currently unable to do because he is banned from entering any football ground. Each day that goes by without him being able to integrate into the team is a waste – both in football and financial terms. The Barça camp also want to organise his official presentation at the Nou Camp as soon as possible.

CAS hands down its verdict on 14 August. The ban remains in force, although he is permitted to exercise with the team and play in friendlies. Which means he'll get to play in front of the home crowd in the Joan Gamper Trophy against Mexican side León. It's a victory of sorts for El Pistolero and the club.

The following day, one month and four days after his transfer, he joins his first training session with his teammates. And he is relieved: 'It was a situation that was making me uncomfortable. I am paying for my mistake and I have apologised, but we need to move past it now.'

At last, on 18 August he goes out onto the pitch in a Barça shirt. It is not his presentation – he is sharing the pitch with the whole team and the new coach, and Messi gets more cheers and applause than he does. But at least he gets to make his appearance after fighting so hard for it.

Meanwhile, Barça trounce their opponents 6-0 in the Joan Gamper. Messi and Neymar both score, but Suárez's performance is uninspiring and he is substituted by Rafinha in the 73rd minute. It's hardly surprising: he hasn't even had a chance to train with the team, let alone familiarise himself with their playing style.

Twenty-four hours later, he attends his first press conference, where he affirms that joining the squad is 'a dream'. He seems happy with the reception he has had from the rest of the team. And he reveals a secret: the previous day's match was not his first at the Nou Camp. 'I have been here many times because I used to enjoy coming and watching them play. I was here at the 5-0 win against Real, the 4-1 victory over Arsenal ... it was lovely coming and enjoying the atmosphere. Now I'm really proud to be here and I just have to take advantage of every opportunity Barcelona has given me.'

Then it's time for some questions from the press.

Why did you choose to play for Barça?
'It's been a dream of mine for years. Everyone knows my wife's connection to this city. I've been thinking about it for a very long time, but I never imagined it would happen. When I realised it was a possibility I wanted it more than anything else. I have fulfilled a dream that I have had since I was very young.'

How does it feel to be the club's newest star?
'Stars are something you see in the sky. I'm just here to help.'

Have you set yourself any targets?
'I have come here to do my best for the team. I'm a forward and I like to score goals. I hope that when I get the chance to make a contribution, I'll be able to score goals or make assists.'

What will your role be in the squad?
'I'm prepared to play in any attacking position. At

Liverpool I played a lot on the left and the right because the number 9 was Sturridge's position. I have no problem adapting to whatever the coach wants or the team needs.'

Are you ready for the challenges that come with being in a team full of exceptional players?
'Leo and Neymar's abilities are incredible, admirable. They deserved so much applause yesterday. I really want to do my bit and win titles. I have played in Europe for many years but still haven't won anything big. I never imagined I would walk in the footsteps of the amazing strikers who have played here. I have to treasure that, and never forget everything I've been through to get here.'

What are your first impressions?
'It's so exciting to share an attacking line-up and a dressing room with players of the calibre of Leo and Neymar and the others. We will do everything we can to win titles. We are not just one or two players, we are a team made up of everyone who goes onto the pitch and everyone on the sidelines as well. What struck me is the amazing atmosphere in the dressing room. The last four days have been really special. They have really welcomed me.'

He goes on to talk about the fallout from the bite, acknowledging that he was afraid the scandal would jeopardise the signing. 'Of course I was worried about the transfer. And I was worried about myself, about what I had done. It's in the past now, I am trying to move past it, to not think about it anymore and just focus on the present. The lesson that I have to carry with me is that I have to be very careful of my actions, and try to forget about it.' He admits that he felt 'depressed' for a while and 'didn't feel like doing anything', although he has received help from 'the appropriate professionals'.

According to reports, the club has entrusted him to psychologists. He arrived with signs of anxiety and stress, and they were said to be concerned about his emotional stability. The media claim that the specialists are also trying to find an explanation for his actions on the pitch.

As the weeks go by, he continues his training, and in mid-September he plays for the reserves in a friendly against the Indonesian Under-19 team, where he scores two of the team's six goals. But it's his weight, rather than his goals, that is attracting attention. As happened with Ronaldinho back in the day, a few journalists are starting to comment that El Pistolero is overweight. At a press conference, coach Luis Enrique is incredulous. 'Suárez, fat? He is a naturally stocky player. He is at his ideal weight.' Then in a more relaxed tone, he says that he hasn't noticed any change since Luis played at Liverpool. 'If you want, we'll give him liposuction, but I don't think he needs it,' he jokes.

It will be a recurring theme for the next few weeks. But fortunately, by 15 October everyone turns their attention back to his goal-scoring abilities, as he collects the European Golden Shoe for being Europe's top scorer, joint with Cristiano. As he holds his trophy, he insists he is '100 per cent ready' for his Barcelona debut.

He will only have to wait a few more days. His first official outing in a Blaugrana shirt will be on Saturday 25 October at 6.00pm at the Santiago Bernabéu. He is making his debut in the first big *Clásico* of the season. It's quite an initiation.

His family are in the stands to support him in this crucial match. Despite four months of inactivity, Luis Enrique has given him a vote of confidence by putting him in the starting line-up. During the few minutes of warm-up time he practises passing with Messi and Ney. They switch positions and take some shots at goal. The Barça attacking trio are finally united and ready to show everyone what they can do.

And it only takes them three minutes. Suárez gets the ball on the right wing and makes an incredible pass to the far side, setting it up perfectly for the Brazilian. It's 0-1, and it's one of the fastest-ever goals in the history of the encounters between the two teams.

A few minutes later, he feeds the ball to Messi,

whose shot is denied by Real goalie Íker Casillas. After that, Barça deteriorate and Madrid take back the game with goals from Cristiano Ronaldo, Pepe and Karim Benzema. With the scoreline against them, Luis seems to find another burst of energy, but the team as a whole seems to be sagging, and he is substituted in the 68th minute. He comes off, knowing that he can do a lot better. The *Clásico* is just a setback. There is still an entire season ahead.

Acknowledgements

I would like to thank Duncan Heath, Philip Cotterell, Robert Sharman, Michael Sells, Sheli Rodney, Estela Celada, Laure Merle d'Aubigné and Roberto Domínguez.

Dedicated to Olmo, Lorenzo, Elvira, Alda and Tullio.